Oscar Michelsen

**Cannibals Won for Christ**

a story of missionary perils and triumphs in Tongoa, New Hebrides

Oscar Michelsen

**Cannibals Won for Christ**
*a story of missionary perils and triumphs in Tongoa, New Hebrides*

ISBN/EAN: 9783337314071

Printed in Europe, USA, Canada, Australia, Japan

Cover: Foto ©Lupo / pixelio.de

More available books at **www.hansebooks.com**

ALL RIGHTS RESERVED.

# CANNIBALS WON FOR CHRIST:

### A Story of Missionary Perils and Triumphs in Tongoa, New Hebrides.

BY

## Rev. OSCAR MICHELSEN,

*Missionary of the Presbyterian Church of Otago, N.Z.*

WITH INTRODUCTION BY

### LIEUTENANT G. C. FREDERICK, R.N.,

*Hydrographic Department, Admiralty.*

LONDON: MORGAN AND SCOTT,
OFFICE OF The Christian,
12, PATERNOSTER BUILDINGS, E.C.

*And may be Ordered of any Bookseller.*

EVERY THURSDAY.          ONE PENNY.

# The Christian:

### A RECORD OF CHRISTIAN LIFE AND TESTIMONY, EVANGELISTIC EFFORT,
### AND
### MISSIONARY ENTERPRISE.

THE object of The Christian is to provide the Church of God with accounts of work done for the extension of the Redeemer's Kingdom in various parts of the world. To earnest toilers at home and to lonely missionaries abroad The Christian has proved a welcome visitor. The Publishers frequently receive from readers in foreign lands hearty testimonies to the encouragement and blessing conveyed to them through its pages; the Portraits and Biographic Sketches given week by week, as well as the numerous accounts of Christian effort at home, and the general Evangelistic Intelligence from various parts of the globe, being heartily appreciated.

LONDON: MORGAN & SCOTT, 12, PATERNOSTER BUILDINGS, E.C.

*And may be Ordered of any Bookseller in the Kingdom.*

## PREFACE.

IT was in response to the repeated solicitations of friends at the Antipodes and in Europe that I decided, during a visit to England, to give an outline of the Lord's work as committed to my hands. Some difficulty arose in the matter, in consequence of all my diaries having been left at the mission station on Tongoa. So this volume is but a statement from memory of some of the many incidents leading up to the condition of things which suggested the title—"CANNIBALS WON FOR CHRIST."

It was not my intention, when this purpose took shape in my mind, to remain more than a few days in England. I was therefore compelled to communicate my story to a friend, whose writings have long been read with acceptance by the Christian public. Finding it possible, however, to return to Great Britain after a brief stay in Norway, I was enabled to contribute several substantial sections to the work, and thoroughly to revise the whole.

At the end of the book will be found an Appendix, which though by no means giving a history of Christian work on the Islands, is intended to afford some idea of the state of missionary effort in the New Hebrides. This must not be looked upon as an exact account of each mission station; but, to the best of my ability, with the information at my command, I have endeavoured to outline the work of my respected fellow-labourers, past and present, on the Islands.

While these pages were passing through the press, my faithful and devoted partner in the mission was called to her rest. This event, so saddening to me, will cause great mourning when it becomes known on the island of Tongoa; whither I hope, in due course, to return to resume my much-loved work.

It is my earnest prayer that the following chapters may stimulate many in the Christian Church to put more implicit faith in God's promises with regard to the spread of the Gospel; and to entertain higher expectations as to the establishment of the Kingdom of God in the dark places of the earth.

OSCAR MICHELSEN.

# CONTENTS.

|  |  | PAGE |
|---|---|---|
|  | INTRODUCTION | 9 |
| I. | TONGOA, PAST AND PRESENT | 13 |
| II. | THE MISSIONARY TO TONGOA | 18 |
| III. | THE FIELD SURVEYED | 28 |
| IV. | MAKING FRIENDS | 40 |
| V. | PROGRESS UNDER DIFFICULTIES | 50 |
| VI. | JOYS AND SORROWS | 57 |
| VII. | A FLIGHT FOR LIFE | 66 |
| VIII. | NEW MISSION QUARTERS | 72 |
| IX. | CANNIBALS RESCUED FROM CANNIBALS | 79 |
| X. | ANOTHER CHANGE OF LOCALE | 85 |
| XI. | DAY BY DAY ON TONGOA | 90 |
| XII. | AN UNEXPECTED CLOUD | 104 |
| XIII. | CANNIBALISM AND ITS HORRORS | 112 |
| XIV. | THREE TONGOAN MARTYRS | 115 |
| XV. | NATIVE SUPERSTITIONS: A RELIGION OF DREAD | 118 |
| XVI. | TWO WRECKS: A CONTRAST | 125 |
| XVII. | HOW TONGOAN CHRISTIANS DIE | 128 |
| XVIII. | SOME TONGOAN "INSTITUTIONS" | 133 |
| XIX. | A QUESTION OF CUSTOM | 142 |
| XX. | PRESENT CONDITION OF THE MISSION | 146 |
| XXI. | THE QUEENSLAND KANAKA TRAFFIC | 153 |
| XXII. | NOTES AND INCIDENTS | 157 |

APPENDIX—

|  | THE NEW HEBRIDES MISSION | 173 |
|---|---|---|
|  | THE ISLANDS AND THE PEOPLE | 184 |

# List of Illustrations.

|  | PAGE |
|---|---|
| PORTRAIT OF REV. OSCAR MICHELSEN. *Frontispiece.* | |
| PORTRAIT OF REV. PETER MILNE | 23 |
| THE WILLIAMS RIVER, ERROMANGA | 32 |
| HEATHEN "DRUMS" | 36 |
| THE MISSIONARY'S "GUN" | 41 |
| TONGOANS (PÉLÉ MEN) AS HEATHEN | 51 |
| MANAMBALEA PREACHING PEACE AT PÉLÉ | 60 |
| THE WOULD-BE MURDERERS LYING IN WAIT | 67 |
| FIRST MISSION HOUSE AT SELEMBANGA | 73 |
| NEW MISSION STATION, SELEMBANGA | 74 |
| MARIPAU, ONE OF MANAMBALEA'S BROTHERS | 80 |
| MARITARILIU AIMING AT THE MISSIONARY | 86 |
| ORIGINAL MISSION BUILDING AT PANITA | 88 |
| ROAD-MAKING ON TONGOA | 94 |
| BUSH SCHOOL HOUSE, EUTA, TONGOA | 99 |
| PORTRAIT OF THE LATE MRS. MICHELSEN, WITH THIRD CHILD | 105 |
| NEW HEAD STATION AT LUMBUKUTI | 147 |
| A GROUP OF CHRISTIAN CHIEFS | 149 |
| MISSION CHURCH AT NGUNA | 180 |

# INTRODUCTION.

N account of what is being done in a far-away corner of the earth, and the story of one who has nobly elected to go forth and preach the Gospel to islanders steeped in savage heathenism, must necessarily be of deep interest to faithful followers of our Lord Jesus Christ. At the same time, it must commend itself to those who wonder why any one should take the trouble to leave home to teach savages. Consequently, such a narrative as that of my dear friend, Mr. MICHELSEN, needs but little introduction; it speaks for itself in all its simplicity. It relates the wonderful dealings of a loving Father, who can keep a single servant of His unharmed, though surrounded by savages thirsting for his blood; who would stop at nothing in the accomplishment of their object, were it not that there is One who can restrain the fierceness of man, and make it turn to His praise.

In addition to the account of his missionary labours, Mr. Michelsen gives an interesting description of the islands he has visited, and their inhabitants. People living in the midst of a nineteenth century civilization can hardly realize the condition of these benighted heathen, sunk in superstition, and practising the most horrible cruelties; so that a narrative by one who has met them in their own haunts must be very instructive. Many who live at home in comfort and ease know little of the trials and privations, as well as dangers, which those have to suffer who follow the promptings and callings of an inner voice, and are ready to say, "Here am I, send me." Accounts of how brave missionaries live in constant expectation that a cruel club, poisoned arrow, or bullet, may end their earthly life while preaching "on earth peace, goodwill towards men," seem to them but idle and exaggerated tales.

Some who have met the missionaries in their distant homes, in houses which their own hands have built, and gazed upon the beautiful scenery, and enjoyed the fine climate, do not realize the isolated life—years spent away from friends and kindred, with only natives to converse with, except on rare occasions—the disappointments encountered, the difficulties to be overcome, and the hardships to be borne. Such may come back and report that the missionaries have a splendid time of it, and after all, do not accomplish much good among the natives! But others, who look into matters, see how wonderfully the Gospel is making its way, surely if slowly; how the natives are learning to worship the Creator, and have faith in His blessed Son; how gladly all trials and difficulties are borne, if only they may be used in fulfilling the Master's command to go forth and "preach the Gospel to every creature."

Having spent many months among the New Hebrides, I can speak from experience as to the change that has come over the inhabitants of some of these islands, and how fully this book deserves its title. Before leaving Australia for the Group, many of my friends, who had some years previously visited the New Hebrides, warned me to be careful in my dealings with the natives, as they were warlike and treacherous cannibals, amongst whom it would not be safe to land without

## Introduction.

being well armed. But what a change did we find had taken place in the vicinity of the missionaries—especially on Tongoa and the neighbouring islands! Cannibalism was quite a thing of the past, and villages were living at peace with one another; they had disposed of all their weapons, so that it was difficult to find any to purchase even as curios—perhaps, rather to our disappointment, as we had quite looked forward to turning our homes in distant England into small museums on our return.

As we walked about from village to village, quite unarmed, we were most hospitably received by the inhabitants, who provided us with such food and refreshment as lay in their power. We found everywhere peace, happiness, and merry faces, where only a few years previously, cruelty, bloodshed, and almost perpetual war, were the common practice. It is well known that savages are proverbially thieves, showing a great amount of cunning and cleverness in appropriating other people's property. By way of giving an example of the good fruit which Christian teaching is producing, I will mention one instance out of many that came under our observation.

During our surveying operations, a boat belonging to H.M.S. *Dart* was swamped by a heavy surf on the south coast of Epi, just opposite Mr. Michelsen's station on Tongoa; the officer and crew having to rejoin the ship some miles further along the coast, where a break in the reef allowed of communication with the shore. Until the weather moderated, nothing could be done towards the recovery of the boat, and all that was in it. About a week later the ship returned to the scene of the accident; and there we found the boat, which had been hauled up on the beach by the natives, and most of the belongings, such as masts, sails, instruments, etc., carefully collected, and piled up near it. As the village was some distance off, the natives had written a message, in their own language, on one of the planks. On interpretation, this ran as follows:—"We have picked up all the things we could find. We have stolen nothing." This, we found, was quite true. The ropes and sails of the boat must have been a great temptation to the natives; but they had learned better, and put into practice what they had been taught.

Without wishing to take up too much space, I must just mention one more incident that took place off Tongoa Island some time after Mr. Michelsen had left for England, on furlough, in 1891. A number of natives came on board the *Dart* one day, some forty or fifty of them, and by way of returning some of their hospitality, we provided refreshment, in the shape of ship's biscuit, with a thick layer of jam (they dearly love anything sweet), and plenty of tea well sweetened. All had been well provided for; but we noticed that not one of them began to eat—they looked as if they were waiting for something. After an awkward pause, it was explained to me that they were waiting for some one to say Grace. I accordingly requested the Chief Tinabua to ask a blessing, which he did in the native language; while all present behaved most reverently, responding with a loud "Amen." Then they set to with a will, and astonished us with their appetites. It was a sight and experience not easy to forget—these dusky islanders, once heathen and cannibals, thanking the Creator of all things for their daily food!

Let us hope that Mr. Michelsen may long be spared to continue his labours among the heathen, and help to hasten that time when "the earth shall be filled with the knowledge of the Lord, as the waters cover the sea."

G. C. FREDERICK.

*Kingsbury,*
    *Middlesex.*

# CANNIBALS WON FOR CHRIST.

## CHAPTER I.

### Tongoa, Past and Present.

Volcanic History of the Island—Warlike Propensities of Early Settlers—Physical Features of Tongoa—A Moral and Spiritual Revolution.

ABOUT 350 years ago, so says tradition, when all seemed to be peace and safety, swift destruction came upon the inhabitants of a large island in Western Polynesia. The natives of the various villages had gone forth to their plantations, or were engaged in their ordinary occupations. Hard labour was the woman's share: she carried in a basket on her back the yams which were required for planting, and in her hand the indispensable firebrand;* while on her neck, or tied in a mat in front of her, was the helpless infant.

The men walked proudly on before with bows and

---

\* Until the introduction of matches, the natives made fire by rubbing together two pieces of wood. This being a rather tedious undertaking, they usually carried with them a firebrand to the plantation for lighting the fire to consume brushwood, or at which to roast a yam.

arrows—some of these plain arrows for shooting birds; others poisoned, to be directed upon their enemies. Clubs and spears were also among their weapons, for use, should occasion offer, in taking human prey; and each man felt himself in a position to defy all opponents.

Suddenly there was an alarming subterranean report, accompanied by a violent earthquake. The shock was prolonged into an irregular vibration, and the explosive roar was continued day after day. No longer did the proud savage reason, in the style of Lamech of old, and think how manfully he would spear and club his foe if he had but the opportunity. The cry of the fearless warrior was the same as that of the affrighted mother and child, and it was—"Whither shall we flee for our lives?"

In the case of multitudes of people all hopes were disappointed and the worst fears realized. Slowly but surely large tracts of land sank into the sea, and other parts of the earth's crust were raised several hundred feet. At three different places fountains of fire were opened up, and glowing lava sprang into the air to an appalling height.

The principal remaining portion of the large island which was thus sundered and destroyed is to-day called Epi, or Api. At the time of which we write, many of the natives whose lot it was to find themselves on the hills which now formed new islands in the sea—one of which is TONGOA—were killed by falling stones, stifled with the prevailing smoke, or burned to death in their hiding-places in the forests; which, in turn, were speedily obliterated by the advancing flames. In some cases all

## Early Settlers.

life, vegetable and animal, was destroyed; and luxuriance and animation gave place to death and barrenness.

In these islands, even to the present day, there are no snakes, although reptiles are very common in other islands in the same region. This fact is corroborative of the native story of the complete desolation wrought by the catastrophe. Moreover, there are evidences, not only of volcanic operations in the past, but of such destructive processes being still at work. There are in Tongoa hot places on which the natives cook their food; and several spots where man cannot tread and vegetation will not flourish.

The several hilltops of the rent and sunken land are now small islands, and are called Tongoa, Tongariki, Buninga, Ewose, Laika, and Tevala. Collectively they were named the "Shepherd Group" by the renowned Captain Cook, and are situated about the middle of the New Hebrides, of which they are a part. The largest of these is designated after Tongo, who is said to have been the first man to settle upon its inhospitable soil, when the volcanic troubles just described had passed by. He was a native of Makura, an island about fourteen miles distant, and a venturesome and enterprising man. Some time afterwards other settlers arrived: first from Emac, a neighbouring island; and later on from Efate, about thirty miles away.

The authority of chiefs was claimed by the leaders of the several expeditions, which resulted in the speedy population of the island; and these chiefs, who adopted the names of the rulers in the villages from which they severally came, have to-day successors who perpetuate their name as well as authority. There was room enough for all on Tongoa, and the land brought forth abundantly to satisfy their needs; but quarrelsome propensities were not kept under control, and the sad fact must be stated that, during ten generations now past—or about 300 years—hardly a single chief on Tongoa has left behind him a peaceful record. History has been largely made up of friendly gatherings alternating with fierce wars and cannibal feasts. Though called *natamate* (peace), and supposed to remove all discord, tribal feasts have been generally followed by fights; and not infrequently have "peace feasts" been got up in order to furnish occasions for hostile attacks upon too-confiding guests.

The Shepherd Group lies to the south-east of Epi, nearly 17 degrees south latitude, and about 169 degrees east longitude. Generally, the islands are exceptionally fertile, especially Tongoa; the extent of which is upwards of twenty square miles. The climate is good, considering the tropical latitude; and, though common throughout the group, malarial fever is rarely experienced on Tongoa. The products include: roots—yam of every description, mountain taro, sweet potatoes, arrowroot, and manioca; fruits—bananas and plantains in great variety, and pine apples. Of indigenous fruit-trees, the most important are the cocoanut palm, bread-fruit, and horse-chestnut. There are also many edible fruits of no commercial value. Of imported fruit-trees, oranges, lemons, custard apples, and mango are the most valuable. The exports are confined to copra (dried cocoa-nut) and a small quantity of maize.

The people of Tongoa are amongst the healthiest and best-looking natives in the New Hebrides. Although principally Efatese, they are taller, stronger, and lighter in colour than their ancestors. This, doubtless, is due to the absence of fever, abundance of food, and a considerable importation of Malay blood from the neighbouring island of Emae. Calling themselves black, they are in reality of a nut-brown shade, with frizzy hair. They are distributed in some ten villages—two in the interior, called "the Bush," and the others near the coast. The houses are of grass, thatched upwards to a ridge pole, surmounting arched pieces of wood, securely settled in the ground. Nowhere in the entire group are there larger or more comfortable residences. The domestic animals are pigs, fowls, and dogs.

Tongoa has, during recent years, been the scene of a moral and spiritual revolution, no less remarkable and complete than that physical change which has just been outlined. Succeeding pages will unfold the story in detail, and relate how peace and goodwill have begun to reign where hatred and warfare were once reckoned among the rights and privileges of humanity. To say that the Gospel of Christ has been instrumental of this mighty change is a true anticipation of what remains to be written.

## CHAPTER II.
## The Missionary to Tongoa.

Early Life in Norway — Emigration to New Zealand — From Commercial Life to Colportage Work—Missionary Aspirations Realized—Departure for the New Hebrides—A Year's Residence at Nguna—Visit to Tongoa, and Subsequent Settlement.

OSCAR MICHELSEN, the missionary who has been privileged to evangelize the Tongoans, is a native of Norway, having been born in 1844. His childhood was spent in the parish of Ski, where his father was sheriff. He was educated for commercial life—a good drilling in foreign languages doing much to stimulate his desire to see lands beyond the Scandinavian Peninsula.

An intellectual father and a sympathetic mother carefully nurtured a large family, but did little or nothing to develop the spiritual life. The general teaching of the National Church at that time had much to do with this neglect; for the religious duties of parents did not go beyond seeing that their children were baptized and confirmed. These things attended to, all was well, if the communion wine and wafer were received before death. "Ye must be born again" suggests to evangelical Christians a body of teaching which was sadly neglected in Norway at that time.

While still a lad, Oscar made the opening verses of Psalm xxxii. the prayer of his heart; and he realized in some measure the blessed consciousness of transgression forgiven and sin covered. But until he was twenty-two years old, he knew little of peace of soul: black world-clouds, with occasional rays of heavenly light, made up the story of his spiritual life. A teacher under whom he studied English, advised him to read a chapter of the English New Testament every evening—an exercise which he found profitable in more ways than one. But, engaged in a business house, and surrounded by worldly influences, he gave little continuous thought to his spiritual welfare.

Two friends of the family having resolved to go to New Zealand, he proposed to accompany them; and his brother, Nicolai Christian, in whose wisdom he had every confidence, not only consented to this course, but generously made it possible. Writing of this period, Mr. Michelsen says:

"Before leaving my native country, I came in contact with several living Christians who influenced me greatly; and I have no doubt their prayers went with me. My limited means did not allow of travelling in the same cabin as my worldly companions. This was my good fortune rather than otherwise; for instead of their society, I had that of two elderly Scotch ladies, the Misses Edgar, who were going to join a brother in Australia. I found in them true friends, of a calm, solid faith, such as I had not known among my acquaintances at home. I have no doubt that my contact with them went far to develop my spiritual life.

"We arrived at Melbourne in June, 1867. I then learned that one of my friends had decided to stay there for a time, and that the other intended to proceed to Queensland. I had no reason, however, to alter my original purpose, so at Melbourne we parted—never again to meet on earth. I arrived in New Zealand, armed with a letter of introduction to a countryman of mine, who 'regretted very much that he could do nothing for me.' I had only money sufficient to provide for one week's board. When my last shilling had been spent, I secured work."

This was in the business establishment of a man having a good reputation for uprightness, although of no religious convictions. His wife was a decided Christian, and greatly grieved that, in common with other tradesmen in the town, her husband kept his shop open on the Lord's Day. Still influenced by Continental ideas regarding the Day of Rest, young Mr. Michelsen saw no objection to this practice; but soon his eyes were opened to Christian obligations and privileges, and he gave notice to terminate his engagement. His services were however retained, with immunity from Sunday duty; his wages also being increased by his appreciative employer, who, a short time afterwards—regardless of the ways of other shopkeepers—closed his establishments on the Lord's Day! The man afterwards became a servant of Him who is Lord of the Sabbath.

Through circumstances over which he had no control, Mr. Michelsen found himself out of work at the end of his first year's residence in New Zealand. For a considerable period he earned no more than would supply bare necessities; but he was never allowed to experience want. He had, from early days of his settlement at the Antipodes, become connected with the Presbyterians; and was glad when, after seven years' business life in the region of the gold mines, the way opened for engagement in Gospel work under the auspices of the New Zealand Bible, Tract, and Book Society.

This agency was the beginning of colportage work in connection with the institution. Going to the bush, he advocated the claims of the society, and sold books and distributed tracts. He visited distant settlements, and was generally received with kindness by the people. At the diggings his experiences were varied and interesting—meeting with many intelligent and generous men. If outwardly rough, some were hard readers, as well as desperate toilers. This colportage work was a fitting introduction to a missionary career.

After a year and a half, this form of service had to be abandoned, because of its excessive strain upon a somewhat slender constitution. The business of the Society had so developed that there was room for an additional worker at the depôt in Otago; and thither Mr. Michelsen went. While realizing that this was a true Christian service, he set his heart upon something more aggressive. He thus describes the workings of his mind:

"Foreign mission work had been my muffled aspiration ever since the time when I first took a decided stand as a Christian. So long as I was travelling, I found a kind of gratification of this desire; but I had not been long at the depôt before all my old wishes came to me as fresh as ever. I quietly sought to qualify for mission work abroad. I made the acquaintance of a Chinaman, who undertook to teach me Chinese, on condition that I should instruct him in English. We made very good progress.

"Just at this time, the National Bible Society of Scotland advertised for a colporteur to work in China. I wrote my application for the post, and sent it to the post-office. The message boy arrived too late for the outgoing mail, and it was a month before the next. In the meantime, the New Hebrides Mission ship *Dayspring* arrived at Dunedin with two missionaries on board, who earnestly asked my Church to send another worker. The reply was that there was no one to send. A great Sunday-school gathering was held on board, and there I met Rev. Lindsay Mackie, who had long been my kind and wise counsellor.

"I said, 'I begin to think of these islands.' He replied, 'That is exactly what I have been expecting. It would suit you far better than that undertaking in China: the prospect of our sending you to China is uncertain; but here is work for which I believe you are fitted, and a man is urgently needed. Write out your application, and I will support it.'

"I wrote my application, and sent it to the then-assembled Synod. My friend warmly supported it; and, as I was well known to nearly all the ministers of the Church through my colportage work, I was readily accepted. After undergoing such training as was thought necessary, I was sent down to the Islands in

1878, with the expressed wish that I should spend a year at Nguna with Rev. Peter Milne, before assuming the responsibility of an independent station."

Rev. Peter Milne was the first missionary of the Otago Presbyterian Church. He is still in the field, and is now gathering in a rich harvest as the reward of faithful service extending over nearly a quarter of a century. At Nguna, while learning a language which was to prove useful in future years, Mr. Michelsen rendered such help as was possible to Mr. Milne. In the early part of the year, the two missionaries visited Tongoa, the younger man being much struck with its beach of black iron-sand ; and the entire island, so far as could be seen, covered with green forest.

REV. PETER MILNE.

It is not a flat coral island, as these specks of land are often supposed to be, but an endless number of hills, some only 400 or 500 feet ; others rising to a height of 1500 or 1600 feet. The sight was beautiful in the extreme. The trees—varied in shade and form—included the horse-chestnut, with its glossy foliage ; the breadfruit, with its light green jagged leaves ; crotons of every imaginable colour ; and banyan-trees, like forest giants, some of them covering an acre.

From the extending branches of these magnificent

trees,* roots are sent down to the ground, enlarging as well as invigorating the tree. Again, from the branches of the banyans were hanging convolvuli and other creeping flowers; whilst ferns and orchids of every description found shelter on branches as well as the trunks. Thus, plants which could not live on the earth, depended upon the monarch tree for existence. All over the hills were seen cocoa-nut palms, with their light-coloured foliage waving in the breeze.

At the very summit of what may be called mountain-tops were tree-ferns, which looked like palms, with the exception that they were of a much darker hue. In Mr. Michelsen's own words:

"The whole scene was delightful beyond description. It wanted but one thing to complete the picture—that was human life. This element was, however, soon supplied; one native after another walking or bounding to the beach. After but slight preparation, they threw themselves into the sea for a morning bath; and when 'dressed' again, seemed to think of nothing but play—men, women, and children alike.

"As they thus laughed and frolicked, the thought stole over my mind: 'What can I do to improve the apparently happy condition of these children of nature?

---

* The banyan tree begins its existence as a parasite on another tree. Gradually it developes into a considerable growth, and in many cases the original tree withers in its embraces. The banyan, however, continues to flourish, and overshadows some of its largest neighbours. The natives are often reminded that, as some proud tree of the forest carries this seemingly insignificant parasite, and is itself soon sacrificed, so the Word of God is conveyed to the people in earthen vessels which must soon wither and disappear; but "the Word of the Lord abideth for ever."

Am I really wanted here?' The question was intelligently answered when I subsequently took up residence in the island, and saw the inhabitants at a shorter distance.

"Going ashore, we were very heartily received. Ah! the chiefs expected presents, and so they were well behaved. Under the grateful shade of trees, hymns were sung, and the Gospel message briefly explained. In the afternoon we rowed round the rock to the north of the Lumbukuti landing, on the west coast of the island. Some bush people were seen, and then lost sight of; villagers were afterwards heard to cry out, *Man-ni-bus* (bush-men). Others were seen with painted faces, wearing black war-plumes in their hair, and with long flowing calicoes hanging from their loins. They looked more picturesque, but not less dangerous, than the Lumbukuti people that had been seen in the forenoon.

"We were conducted to an open space, about half a mile in the interior of the island, by Tarisaliu, a dashing chief, fully six feet in height; he was dressed in a white European suit, and quite 'got up' for the occasion. All the time his heathenism showed itself in a pair of pigs' tusks, which dangled at the end of locks of hair on each side of his face, which still had traces of paint upon it. In savage fashion, his long frizzy hair had been coiffured with lime, and tied up in a bunch on the top of his head. Surmounting the whole was a pretty yellow straw hat, which was often thrown off when touched by branches of trees, and promptly replaced by an attendant. Of these incidents the chief was quite unconscious, for the hat was but a roof on the heavy stack of hair which his noble head sustained."

An old heathen drum was standing on the place of meeting, which had once been a dancing ground, but was now almost covered with scrub. Tribes had been at war, and the scene wore the complexion of desolation. The story of life from the dead was told, and some Christian songs were sung. On all hands were to be seen the fruits of sin ; so it was with real appropriateness that the only regenerating power for a lost world was proclaimed. Passing through deep valleys, shaded by high trees, and everywhere luxuriant with ferns, the missionaries observed a beautiful knoll, which was pointed out as the site from which a tribe known as the Pélé people had been driven further inland by their powerful neighbours of Lumbukuti.

Approaching the village of Pélé, a war-fence, or *páké*, such as were once common in the island, was seen. The chief of the village, named Marimaraki, a blunt, harsh-looking man, with a tuft of hair from a pig's tail in each ear, was met. He was known to have been in New Caledonia, so Mr. Michelsen addressed him in French. The short answer of the distinguished traveller was in the pigeon-English of the South Seas : " Me no savez that talk ; me talk all de same as you ! "

In acknowledgment of presents to natives, the missionaries received yams and cocoa-nuts ; and left for Nguna with definite impressions of the needs of Tongoa and the prospects of work there.

All the chiefs on Tongoa seemed friendly to missionaries on the occasion of the visit of Messrs. Milne and Michelsen. One went so far as to invite the latter to settle at his village; but there was afterwards reason to believe that he only wanted to have a *tapu* (sacred) power to stand between himself and stronger tribes.

As the time approached for Mr. Michelsen to leave Nguna for Tongoa, he was down with "island" or intermittent fever, and momentarily expected to die. It was thought by his friends on Nguna that nothing but a sea voyage in the Mission ship, soon to start for Sydney, would save his life. In due course however, according to arrangement, the Mission ship arrived, with Revs. H. A. Robertson and D. Macdonald, two missionaries labouring in other islands, who had come to assist in the settlement of Mr. Michelsen on Tongoa. "It's only fever," they said; "and we have all had that."

"It is but a question of dying here or there," reasoned Mr. Michelsen; and the point was not worth debating. So the arrangements were duly carried out.

Arrived at Tongoa, the two missionaries, assisted by sailors and natives, erected a frame-and-plaster house for the new worker, who was so weak that he could not walk alone up to his station.

After nine days the ship left, and Mr. Michelsen found himself a solitary white man, a Christian, in a population of about eleven hundred cannibal heathens! Was he cast down? No; he remembered his God! What about dying? He thought no more of it; but, with a courage implanted and sustained by Divine grace, he addressed himself to the work which he had undertaken in the name of Christ.

## CHAPTER III.

### The Field Surveyed.

Dealings with Tongoan chiefs—"We are afraid of you!"—First Impressions and Experiences—Matabuti's Welcome—A Sabbath Preaching Tour—Threatened by a "sacred" chief.

THIS section, which involves a slight retrogression, is given in the missionary's own words :

Our little party sailed north, a distance of 30 miles, from Nguna to Tongoa during the night, and suddenly we found ourselves under lee of the island. The natives, with their merry *o-ah! o-ah! o-ah!* were bounding down on the dark strand, and natural beauty made the landscape lovely beyond imagination.

With these scenes before me, new hopes were a-wakened. Thinking of these poor heathen, who for the moment seemed so merry, but whose life I thoroughly knew was a ceaseless slavery in the service of the enemy of souls, I was gradually drawn out to pray that the Lord would give me two years of active service among them, so that I might preach the Gospel in every village. Though I could hardly expect to live to see the people changed from a heathen to a Christian community, I felt sure that, if I were but allowed to proclaim the message of salvation to them, God would bless his own Word; and I would see the fruit in eternity, if not in time.

The previous day, racked with fever, I thought of little else but dying—an event which I believed to be very near. The Lord had now inspired me with faith and hope for future usefulness. I thought no more of dying; but was fully determined to go forward in the strength of the Lord to do his work.

Some native Christians from other islands accompanied Messrs. Robertson and Macdonald and myself. We landed, as before, on the west side of the island, on which there were but two villages, one large and the other very small. No other part was so fit for a mission station. Immediately on landing I asked for Malakaleo, the chief of Lumbukuti, the larger village. He soon presented himself, and did not favourably impress me. A stout, gross-looking man, his eyes bore testimony to his strong animal instincts. A load of white beads, several pounds in weight, hung round his neck; a small whale's tooth served as a nose jewel; a fathom of Turkey twill secured a broad belt of bark to his waist. With various other ornaments, these indicated that the chief aspired to hold a place among the dandies of the island.

Round one of Malakaleo's eyes a black ring had been painted, and round the other a yellow one; a plume of cocks' feathers stood in his lime-besmeared hair, and in one hand he carried a short rifle. These were exhibited as proofs that the chief was a mighty man of war. Finally, a large number of pigs' tusks, borne round the wrist of his favourite wife, served to announce that he was a social power; for all of these were taken from pigs presented to him by chiefs desirous of doing him honour.

This, then, was the man I had to deal with. He smiled graciously when he came down to meet me, and asked at once what I had in the carpet-bag in my hand. "Come up under the trees," I said, "and I will show you." His eyes glistened as I took out a small hatchet and gave him. Then I produced a clearing-knife, *i.e.*, a butcher's knife with a fourteen-inch blade—a useful tool with which to reduce the bush for plantation purposes. I also presented him with a fathom of Turkey twill, and other things highly esteemed by the natives of these islands. He was getting quite demonstrative, and seemed nigh to embracing me.

I then asked if there were any other chiefs present; for I not only wanted to prepare the heart of this all-important personage, but was desirous of doing my best to remove all evil influence. Quite a number of men presented themselves as chiefs. In my own mind I felt—what later experience has proved to be the fact—that these were nearly all "got up for the occasion." However, I had intended to give away all I had in the bag; so if some real chiefs neglected to defend their prerogative for the sake of helping some of their friends, they did so at their own expense. When the bag was empty, I thought the time for action had come.

I turned to Malakaleo, and said, "I would like to live here altogether. Could you not sell me a place at your village, where I could put up my station?" I thought that he would surely like to have such a friend living beside him. The man's countenance fell. He said, hesitatingly, "We are afraid of you." Nothing that I could say was of any avail to move this stern savage. Underneath the rough exterior there was a conscience. He was an ambitious man, who delighted to see his people victorious over their enemies, even if he now and then lost a few of his own men. He also loved to be shown honour at heathen feasts, which he knew I would discourage.

Malakaleo was a vicious cannibal, who, soon after I settled on the island, made use of the expression, "I hunger for human flesh!" To prevent cannibalism, I once sent him a tin of preserved meat. He was a "sacred" chief, who pretended to have power to do many wonderful things. It was perhaps a matter of doubt with him if these powers would bear the light of day. It need hardly be added that he was a thorough sensualist. How would all this agree with Christianity and its representative now standing before him? "Axes, knives, calicoes, beads, etc., were all very good; but—I cannot have this man beside me, and follow my old course." These were his reasonings. Hence his laconic reply, "We are afraid of you."

Should I draw back? If I had the "I am with you" as my strength, surely it would not do to allow such a miserable worldling to stop me! The Lord often bids His people to go forward, but at the same time requires them to stoop. There was yet that other chief of the small village Panita, on the same side of the island. I therefore turned to him. Maritariliu's answer was, "I require some time to think over it."

After more than an hour he returned. Doubtless he

had consulted other chiefs. "Yes, I can sell you a piece of ground for a mission station." We all proceeded up to his place. A native kindly allowed me to lay my elbow on his shoulder, as, with a stick in my right hand, I walked up to the village. When

THE WILLIAMS RIVER, ERROMANGA.

we arrived there, he demanded payment for his services! I felt it would be making a very bad beginning to give him anything; so I told him that I had come there as their *friend*, and if he wanted to be paid for a little kindness like that, it was quite clear that *he* did not wish me to be there; nor did he mean all the words he had spoken to me by the way! He did not press the matter further.

## "Infested with Ghosts!"

The chief of Panita pointed to a ridge as being the spot he would sell. After examination, the land, covering five or six acres, was bought, and well paid for in various kinds of barter—value about £7 or £8.

Clearing was at once commenced. I noticed that the Tongoans, who were quite willing to help, were particularly careful not to touch the precise part where I wished to build the house. They left that to the Efate and Erromanga Christians, who had come with us to help to build.* The fact of the matter was, it was a "sacred place," an old graveyard terribly "infested with ghosts!" It would be a splendid thing to have a missionary there—a man over whom they believed the spirits had no power! His living there would indeed drive away the ghosts, and make the place like the neutral ground around. So the natives reasoned.

My two missionary friends, assisted by sailors from the Mission ship, and "the foreign natives," had the roof on the house in nine days from the time we arrived at the island. The walls were far from "light proof," and there might be divided opinions as to whether the house really was habitable. Being unable to do anything myself, I had to be thankful that the house was as it was.

The Mission ship left on a Saturday, after a stay of nine days. Going ashore for good, I walked along the beach—the only European on the island—to my new

---

\* The Efatese helpers I paid for their work. The Erromangans said they had done it for the Lord, and would have no payment from me!

home, to commence work for the Lord. It was a joyful day.

The next morning I went down to Panita, sang some hymns, and spoke to the people. The language had been acquired during my stay on Nguna. The reception accorded me was kindly. Immediately after the service I was attacked by fever, and was unable to visit neighbouring villages.

During the following week visitors came from all parts of the island, and I spoke and sang to them. All brought produce for sale, and there was a general curiosity as to what I was disposed to give them! The almost universal experience is for the missionary to be well received at first; but when it is realized that his purpose is not simply to bestow temporal advantages, but to insist upon "breaking with sin" as a condition of securing heavenly blessings, the natural man protests. There is, in fact, an entire change of attitude.

On the Tuesday I was down with fever—the second and last attack I had on the island. While in great pain, the native boy from Efate, who had come with me as servant, informed me that a chief was outside desiring to see me. When the worst of the attack was over, I called in the visitor. It was Matabuti, from the village of Meriu, in the south of the island; a quiet-looking man, who spoke deliberately, and seemed to have his thoughts well ordered. He had suffered much. He once had inflammation in one of his eyes, and for want of proper treatment had lost the use of it. He had also been much oppressed by a powerful chief,

Ti-Tongoa; and, like Israel of old, sighed after a deliverer.

Briefly stated, the chief's message of welcome was: "I am very glad you have come. A long time ago I had a wonderful dream. I thought I saw a ladder from earth to heaven, and God sitting at the top. When you came, I knew you were the man that belonged to that ladder. I would like you to come over to our village as often as you can, and tell us all about it."

The man thought I could explain everything—I had come to point them the way to God! And so it was in truth. The incident cheered me very much; not only was the Lord with me, but He had also gone before me, preparing some at least to hear the Gospel.

The following Sunday, the ninth day after landing, the Lord having abundantly heard my prayers for restored health, I felt no more effects of the fever. In the morning I held a small meeting at Panita, and some of the village lads accompanied me to Bongabonga. They led me to the open square of the village, on one side of which was the *farea*—a kava, or cannibal, feast-house.

On the other side of the square was a sacred place, upon which the most conspicuous objects were the skulls and jawbones of persons who had recently been eaten by the villagers. There was also a sacred stone, probably an altar for articles sacrificed to the spirits; and a chest which no one would claim—perhaps it belonged to some one who had died—at all events it was shunned because regarded as ill-omened. The dead man's treasure was left with him—not an uncommon practice.

## The Field Surveyed.

I got one of the natives to beat a drum—a tall, hollow tree trunk erected in memory of the dead—and we had a considerable congregation, who listened attentively to the singing of Gospel hymns, and evinced much interest in the words spoken to them. Nevertheless, in after-time this proved one of the hardest places I had to deal with.

HEATHEN "DRUMS." *

Proceeding to Meriu, I was cordially welcomed by Matabuti, the chief who had had the wonderful dream. He at once brought me some green cocoanuts, that I might refresh myself with the milk; and ordered his wives to kill fowls, get yams, and prepare a great feast.

* See also p. 151.

I promptly stayed his hand, and, to his great disappointment, would only accept the cocoanuts and some cold baked yams. I told him and his people of the Gospel feast, and promised to go again the following Sunday.

At Mangarisu, the village of the quiet but shrewd chief, Ti-Tongoa, the majority of the people were away at their plantations; but we had a small meeting. Proceeding through the bush, we reached, in the afternoon, Lumbukuti, the village of Malakaleo. We found a few men and a number of boys in the open square, and I went into the *farea* and began to sing and speak to an ever-increasing audience.

After a time I heard some very loud talking outside; and bringing my address to a close, I sang the Hundredth Psalm, probably with more earnestness than ever before, as I suspected the noise outside to be an expression of hostility to my mission. In a few minutes I was convinced that my suspicions were well-founded.

Malakaleo and a number of his men were in the square. The chief was busy pouring the milk of a young cocoanut into a hole they had dug in the ground. As already stated, he was a "sacred" chief, recognised as competent to deal with powers unseen; and his act at that moment was an invocation of vengeance upon me, in order to cause my death!

Going up to Malakaleo, I addressed him in the kindliest words; but he maintained a stolid indifference to most of what I said. One thing, however, struck him. It was my remark: "Do not be afraid of Christianity.

God asks you to give up a yam,* and receive a pig!' In other words, I told him that the sacrifice which God demands of His creatures is small in comparison with His unspeakable Gift.

Hearing the word "pig," the chief exclaimed: "Who is willing to give me a pig?" I then explained my illustration; but the benighted man turned a deaf ear to my words, and shook his club at me.

A friendly native from Panita made a sign to me, whereupon I realized the danger of my position, and withdrew a few steps. After some further attempts, all in vain, to get his ear, I left for Panita.

Need I say that on reaching the mission station I thanked my Heavenly Father for having permitted me to witness for the Lord Jesus before so many people in one day. I had walked twelve miles, and delivered five addresses, besides singing Gospel hymns.

In my preaching I told them that Jesus had come into the world—and why. I said: "God has made us; He owns us"—a significant expression among the natives, for ownership should carry obedience. "We have disobeyed the commands of God, and brought upon ourselves His anger. God is angry with us, black man and white man alike. When you are afraid of the anger of the spirits, you make a sacrifice. So a sacrifice has been made to avert the anger of God, and that sacrifice is available for each and all of us. About this I have come to tell you."

---

* Yams are plentiful and of small value compared with pigs, which are held in high esteem; and never overlooked when one chief wishes to compliment another by way of making him a present.

## An Unfortunate Mistake.

When I came to reflect upon that memorable day's proceedings, I realized that I had made an unfortunate mistake. I took upon myself to hold a meeting in Lumbukuti without previously asking the permission of the chief; hence the unpleasant occurrence which I have described. I decided never to do this again. Nor did I ever have occasion to force myself upon the attention of any village, for I always had more congregations willing to listen to the Word than I was able to satisfy.

## CHAPTER IV.
## Making Friends.

A Curious Visitor and his Errand—Tongoan Land Customs—
"How many guns have you?"—Women hear the Gospel—A Chief
"learns to read"—Mendicant Logic on Tongoa—Divine Providence Illustrated—A Blind Man's Joy.

THE missionary shall continue the story :—

Not long after settling on Tongoa a stranger came into the house. He looked as if he had a right there, but at the same time was quite friendly. He was a man of about fifty, and his whole appearance suggested that he was a chief. After looking round in all directions, he said, "You have come to live on my land." I then knew who he was, for I had learned a few days previously that the land I had purchased from Maritariliu was the property of Malai, the real chief of Tongalapa, the place where I lived. He had been driven away from the island many years before.

Malai's chieftainship was called Tonga-lapa-manu, *lapa* is "great," and *manu* is "thousand." This would

THE MISSIONARY'S "GUN."

imply that this *great* chieftainship was spoken of as having a *thousand* of a population. They were in their day feared by all around ; they used to make chase on all and sundry, to kill and eat them. Seeing the power of this common foe, several of the other villages forgot their own petty jealousies, and joined together to crush their dreaded enemy.

The villages of Panita, Malatolu, and Liseiriki, and probably others, joined, and proved too great a power for Malai and his tribe. The people were first driven over the mountain, and settled right in the middle of the island. For some time they were quiet ; but at length showed that they had not changed in disposition, although they had been conquered. The united forces already mentioned again drove Malai and his tribe away. This time he fled to Meriu, where he found shelter for awhile ; but even there he did not feel very safe. He went over to Emac, where he found hospitality at Sasake, a warlike village on the north side of the island. They were only too glad to receive such an addition to their population.

Malai had been a great warrior in his day, and he did not seem to be wanting in cunning. Feeling that he could not safely return to take up his possession on Tongoa, he judged it wise to be civil on his visit to me.

It is the usage among these natives that even if a tribe is driven away, they do not thereby forfeit the ownership of their land. Also, a custom obtains in native warfare that no peace can be made until the victorious tribe has paid damages for excessive injury done to the vanquished enemy ! I knew then that

Malai had a perfect right to order me off the land; and, at any rate, had friends enough in Tongoa to make it very unpleasant for me. So I said I was aware that the land was his, and that I was quite willing to pay him for it. I gave him part payment then, and promised to order from Sydney a grindstone and some other things, which I had not with me then.

Thus I had paid for the land twice—not to mention that Mr. Milne, on a visit to Tongoa years before, had purchased from the great Malakaleo, who, at that time, was a refugee at Panita, a small piece of ground for a mission station, which I afterwards discovered was part of Tongalapa! One would think that the mission had fully established its right to the land by that time!

As a further precaution, on the advice of Rev. Dr. J. G. Paton, I had also put a clause in the deeds that all the *trees* were included in the purchase. Satisfied that I had acquired every right to the place, I sent a boy to gather some cocoanuts, which I required for their milk, to be used as yeast wherewith to make bread. He then told me that he had had trouble with the Panita people about the nuts, as they claimed them as theirs! So I was compelled to climb the cocoanut tree myself.

Next morning I did not neglect to mention the matter in the school. "Yes," they said, "it is quite right." "No," I replied, "it is quite wrong!" I asked them what the barter had been for which Maritariliu had divided between his people. He did not own the land, so that it could only be for the trees! I silenced all for the time, but had afterwards to pay a young man for a cluster of the cocoanut trees, for which he assured me he had received no payment.

About this time a native entered the house flourishing a war-axe. He declared that the mission house had been erected on *his* land. It seemed that he had had a plantation in the place some years previously. He claimed compensation; but was told that he need not expect it, as the land had already been paid for to Malai—and compensation also given to the chief of Panita. I gave him a piece of bread and butter, and commenced a friendly chat. Nothing more was said about compensation.

These circumstances impressed me with the fact that, though fairly trustworthy in dealings among themselves, the natives had been in the habit of regarding strangers as proper persons to be "taken in" when possible.

"How many guns have you?" was a curious inquiry early addressed to me by a party of Lumbukuti warriors. "None," was the reply. This was quite incredible to men who would not dare to leave their village unarmed. Continuing, I admitted the possession of just one gun, and this I showed to my astonished interrogators. Need it be said that it was the one weapon of Christian warfare—the Word of God. "This," I explained, "is the only gun I have; and in course of time it will silence all the others on the island."

It is excusable that at that time the Tongoans should declare the Book without power. They neither knew it as the sword of the Spirit nor the shield of the Lord. To-day a different conviction prevails, for marvels have been wrought in the name of the Prince of Peace.

Within the first month or so all the chiefs called upon me, with the exception of two. Most likely the object

## Inquiring Chiefs. 45

of the visitors was to receive presents. One of the two who did not come was Marimaraki, head of Pélé, the bush village, which was engaged in war at the time. The other was Manambalea, of Selembanga, on the east side of the island. This chief, of which much will be said hereafter, was an energetic and courageous man, rather pleasant in appearance. He had made himself no less distinguished as a warrior than as an organizer of friendly gatherings of the tribes.

Manambalea thought well to inquire concerning the new religion before visiting its teacher, so he despatched some of his people to see what they could learn. Now, a week or two before, while working for me, several men of Selembanga had seen a picture of Jesus at the Well, talking to the woman of Samaria. Accompanied by some women, one of these men turned up at the mission house, saying they wanted "to see Jesus." The picture was shown, whereupon the man exclaimed, "Yes, that is it! That is the Son of God who came into the world to save us from our sins and from hell, and to help us to get to heaven hereafter."

The women evidently thought the man had not got a correct version of the story; so they appealed to me, and I explained the wonderful incident, telling of the love and power of Jesus to save. They had heard enough at home to impel them to walk six miles to learn more; and they went back with the feeling that the half had not been told them.

At length the tardy chief made a personal call, and asked for information. An acquaintance was then formed, which has been fruitful of important results throughout the history of the mission. Not knowing the chief's mind, I began by explaining that I had taken up my abode on the island in order to tell the people the way of salvation. Manambalea seemed greatly astonished at the good news. He attended evening worship in the mission house, and afterwards made no sign of leaving. He ceased not to ask questions concerning the Gospel; and when I set forth the truth in song, the uniform request was "Sing it again!"

At a late hour that evening he was asked to retire to rest, with the prospect of hearing more on the following day. His answer was: "I want to go home in the morning, and tell my intentions to my people; but I will return hither in the afternoon." This he did, coming back to learn to read! At that time no person of importance in the island had taken such a decided stand, except Matabuti at Meriu. Meanwhile, in Malakaleo's quarter, strong words and feelings were prevailing against the Gospel.

Not long afterwards a company of Malakaleo's fighting men appeared at the mission station, probably to inquire about Manambalea's object in staying with me. When they met him, they asked if he intended to work for the missionary. Of course, he would be working there, and it would be the easiest thing in the world to say so, and conceal his real object. "No," he said decidedly, "I have come to 'take the Book,'" *i.e.*, submit to religious instruction.

The tone of his voice was such as to discourage further interrogation. He remained a considerable time

## A Chief Converted.

at the mission house, and made rapid progress in knowledge. It was his real determination from the first to become a Christian; I had to be faithful, and the inquirer had to be honest, or it would not have been possible now to report Manambalca's conversion, and his humble position at the feet of Jesus.

My deliberate judgment is that there is no man on Tongoa who would make the same sacrifices for his Master; nor has any one on the island exerted himself so much for the Redeemer's Kingdom as Manambalca. At times when all others have failed, I have found a faithful friend in him. The story of this brother and his work would almost require a separate volume to do justice to it.

Among the many callers at the mission station were not only those who had produce to sell, but such as wished to honour me, a stranger, by receiving any presents that I might be disposed to give. It was not uncommon in the early days of the mission for a man to present himself at the door with the enigmatical remark, "I love you." What more natural than that, conscious that my resources were distinctly limited, I should say: "When I love any one, I do what I can to make him happy and comfortable. Now, if you love me, why have you not brought me some yams, or a fowl, or something that would prove of service?"

The native beggar, however, not impelled by want, but actuated by the insatiable cry of the horseleech's daughters, said, "Give, give," in terms of the politest compliment! He loved the missionary! Ought not the missionary to make him a present in return? That was the form of mendicant logic on Tongoa! Others again would bring me presents, not because they had a grain of affection for me, but because they expected a more valuable article in exchange.

There came a time, early in the work, when the visitors grew few and far between. The explanation was, that all the presents and barter goods had been disposed of, and a considerable time must elapse before the *Dayspring* would arrive with a fresh supply. In such circumstances as these, God tried my faith. When temporal prospects were very dark, I committed my cares to the Lord. Not many days afterwards, and before we were actually in want, a tribe of natives came along, carrying taro, yams, bananas, and cocoanuts. I was not a little surprised to see them at this time; as, with others, they had lately ceased to come, because they knew I had nothing to buy with. "Well," I said, "you have come; but I have nothing to pay you with."

They replied, "We know that; but these things were sent down to us by Marimaraki, who requested us to bring them over to you as a present."

So our wants were supplied by the least likely man on the island—a man who afterwards showed himself to be of the meanest disposition. The God of Elijah can feed his servants by gifts from a savage black man, as well as by meat conveyed by voracious ravens.

Marimaraki's life throws no light whatever upon his strange act. Years later he asked the missionary how much he would give him to "take the Book." The providential goodness of God fully explains the occurrence, for in His hands the heart of a bush chief is as tractable as that of a highly-civilized ruler.

### A Hearty Welcome.

From quite early days on the island, Mr. Michelsen visited Selembanga. The people always gave him a warm welcome. They showed him what they considered the most interesting object in the village—a remarkably fair-skinned boy, which the wife of the young chief—Manambalea's nephew—had borne to him in Queensland.

They also took him to the house of an old blind man, who was regarded with peculiar interest. The missionary having been introduced as "the man of God," the poor old pilgrim exclaimed, "Oh, is that the man of God? Let me feel him." Laying his trembling hands upon the servant of Christ, he seemed to experience unspeakable satisfaction. His words and actions were in the spirit of the prayer of Simeon of old: "Lord, now lettest Thou Thy servant depart in peace;...for mine eyes have seen Thy salvation."

## CHAPTER V.
## Progress under Difficulties.

Work at the "Sunday House"—The Mission Station Robbed—"A Sign"—Full Restitution, resulting in New Friendships—A Ngunese Christian Chief's Confession—Visit to Emae—Karisi, the Little "Misi."

DURING week-days Mr. Michelsen's time was spent in manifold work for the good of the people: teaching, visiting, etc. On Sundays he would take a preaching tour, and late in the afternoon and evening be "at home" for visitors. Numbers of men and boys, assembling to sing and hear what the missionary had to tell them, made the first day of the week very different from others—not to them only, but to their companions also. Probably on that account the boys of the village called the mission premises the "Sunday House." Among the elements of day-school instruction, Mr. Michelsen included the names of the days of the week in English; and the proceedings at the "Sunday House" did much to impress the important lesson.

## A Band of Thieves. 51

The missionary will speak for himself regarding incidents of this time :—

"Returning home from the Synod that met in the Islands, during the first year of the work on Tongoa, I observed a peculiar strangeness among the people

TONGOANS (PÉLÉ MEN) AS HEATHEN.

They seemed quite friendly, but it was plain that there was something I had yet to learn.

"Approaching the house, I thought I saw a change in its appearance; but I could not tell what was the matter. Just then, one of the natives told me that a band of Malakaleo's men had broken into the place during my absence. They were led by a man from Panita, who, through frequent visits to the mission station, knew how to effect an entrance. They turned over everything; examined every nook and corner; and carried off just anything that struck their fancy.

"I cannot say I took this very much to heart, as I was quite prepared for such occurrences. Changing the subject, however, I told the people I purposed that evening showing them *Navaevaeana*—the 'Sign'—for thus the magic lantern is styled on Nguna. The announcement did not cause nearly so much pleasure as I anticipated. As a fact, my meaning was hardly clear to the people. But, intending to surprise them, I did not stop to explain.

"The news spread rapidly; 'in less than no time,' so to say, it reached the ears of Malakaleo's men, of burglarious notoriety, in Lumbukuti. Then came a message from Tinabua, the young chief, entreating me to send no calamity upon the people; and, furthermore, assuring me that all the things that had been taken away from the mission house should be returned on the following day! I saw no reason, however, to defer my inoffensive magic lantern display.

"The next day Tinabua, accompanied by the senior chief, Malakaleo, their fighting men, and many others, came up to the mission house. They were all armed and painted, as well as decorated with plumes of cocks' feathers. They brought with them axes, knives, pieces of print, and every item of my missing property upon which they could lay their hands.

"I took advantage of the occasion to make Tinabua a present of several of the articles. Acknowledging his honesty, I admonished him to remain a just and upright ruler. I have reason to believe that this little incident went far to make him a firm and constant friend of the mission.

"Another occurrence made a great impression upon the natives. During my absence the Panita men had joined the Lumbukuti warriors against the Pélé people, and the only man shot in the fight was the Panita man who had acted as guide to the burglars!

"During the same year I paid a visit to Nguna, in my boat. Conversing with some of the Christian natives, I told them of the Lord's blessing upon my labours, and of the wonderful manner in which He had opened the way for me to preach the Gospel to the Tongoans. One of the company expressed his surprise, and a second followed suit. After several had made casual remarks, Matakoale, an elderly Christian chief, said : 'I am not at all surprised : further, we should not be surprised. It is just what we have been praying for all the time ; and God has heard our prayers. Let us praise Him!'"

Mr. Michelsen had occasion to go to the island of Emae, to make a settlement of the claim of Malai, the real owner of the land at Panita on which the mission house had been erected. He was received with much kindness by the villagers of Sasake, who had heard of the work on Tongoa from those who had visited the island. In the evening, before retiring to rest, the missionary assembled the Tongoans who had accompanied him, and commenced the usual worship with a hymn. This was not only a novelty, but a great enjoyment, to the natives present ; and before Mr. Michelsen could engage in prayer, the heathen chief demanded a repetition of the hymn. This was not all; for he continued requesting *encores* far into the night, the hymns being explained and the Gospel preached. There is reason to believe that this and other meetings with the Sasake people did much to open their hearts for the Gospel. Since then teachers from Efate have been settled there.

An interesting visitor during the first year at the mission station was a lad named Karisi. His upper lip had been badly cut with a knife used for clearing the bush, and he sought the missionary's surgical aid. The wound was carefully sewn up, and periodically dressed. After some days, the lad proposed to stay at the station and serve Mr. Michelsen in any way he could; and the proposal was gladly accepted.

Karisi at once impressed the missionary favourably, being a tall, spare lad, with thoughtful eye. Though fond of fun, he was all attention to religious instruction. By dint of close application he speedily learned to read, and his whole conduct showed him to be earnestly seeking the truth. One evening, during worship, Mr. Michelsen called upon him to engage in prayer. He knew how anxiously he had taught the youth; but he did not know to what a degree the instruction had been spiritually appropriated. To his joyful surprise, Karisi, with little hesitation, stood up and offered the prayer which the Lord taught His disciples. He afterwards gave unmistakeable evidence of being a truly-converted boy. "How can I keep from singing!" might well be given as his motto. Until late in the evening one would hear from Karisi's hut the strains of one Gospel hymn after another.

No sooner was the youth's interest in the new religion reported to Malakaleo, than that chief devised evil purposes. Mr. Michelsen continues the narrative :—

"In the evening, after I had gone to bed, there was a knock at my door. I asked, 'Who is there?' The answer was, '*Kinau!*' (I !). It was Karisi's voice, and I let him in. In those days I was in the habit of bolting my doors. I have given that up a good while now; things have changed.

"When Karisi entered, I asked what was the matter; and he answered that he had just learned that Malakaleo intended sending up some of his men to kill him—probably that night.

"I told him not to fear. We had trusted ourselves into the hands of the Lord, and He would take care of us. I directed him to sleep in the front room; and in the event of any one coming to the door, not to answer it personally, but to waken me. Then I would go to the door, and he could get under my bed!

"I went to lie down again, expecting Karisi to do the same. I listened for intimations of the arrival of the hostile party. After awhile I thought I heard something like a human voice, and at once concluded that the would-be murderers were approaching. I strained my ears to distinguish the sounds, and then heard more and more clearly the words of song. It was Karisi; and the hymn was the native version of 'My Jesus, I love Thee; I know Thou art mine.' Subsequently the lad engaged in prayer, asking God to preserve our lives, and to touch Malakaleo's heart, and lead him to a knowledge of Jesus. Further, he prayed

God to banish all heathen darkness, and establish His Kingdom on Tongoa.

"That prayer of the little 'misi' (missionary) has been abundantly answered. Karisi's life was saved; and in the case of Malakaleo, the lion has been turned into the lamb by the operation of Divine grace."

Subsequent chapters will show in what remarkable power the Kingdom of Heaven has come to the people of the island.

## CHAPTER VI.
### Joys and Sorrows.

A Lady Missionary—More about the Little "Misi"—A Native Peace-maker—Christianity to be "Stamped out"—Murderous Plots Frustrated.

AT the close of the first year of his work on Tongoa, Mr. Michelsen felt that it was not good for a man to be alone.* Sometimes the solitude had been almost painful to him: he would look at his hands, and long to see white kindred. He returned to New Zealand, seeking a wife as well as a brief respite from the seclusion and anxieties of Tongoa.

Having married Miss Jane Langmuir, of Otago, a lady who for twelve years proved the sharer of his domestic joys and sorrows, as well as a partner in his mission work, he returned to the island in the early part of 1881. The new arrival caused unbounded delight among the native women. They showed their joy by

---

* Through the death in London, at the end of 1892, of his devoted wife, he is again alone. But we must not anticipate this sorrowful bereavement. Chapter XII. will give particulars.

jumping and screeching, as they crowded round the lady missionary on the beach. No reception could have been more warm and hearty.

Mrs. Michelsen little anticipated the trials and difficulties which lay before her. The next thing was to make home comfortable; and in a very short time the little building which then did duty for a manse was rendered bright and cheerful. Since then, to the growing interest of the people, a little family has been added to the home.

One of the first to call upon the missionary after his return to Tongoa, was the loyal Manambalea, with whom the boy Karisi had been left to do his best as "teacher." Mr. Michelsen asked the chief how they had been getting on; and he said, "Very well."

" Have you learned to read?"

" Yes."

" How have you spent your Sundays in my absence?"

" Preaching, of course!"

" What have you been doing on week-days?"

" We have had school daily, and quite a number of villagers have attended."

Manambalea added that the Sunday work began with services held in his village, and afterwards extended from village to village on his side of the island. The chief himself beat the drum and called the people together; and then, after a few words, he introduced Karisi to sing and preach. The deep piety of this lad has already been described. Doubtless his endeavours during the absence of the missionary were an important preparation for aggressive work such as was engaged in afterwards.

## "A Very Bad Lot."

Manambalea had, however, something to tell that was not of so pleasing a character. During the missionary's absence fresh war had broken out; and the villages had united in a proposal to exterminate the people of Pélé, one of the two bush villages. Manambalea explained that the Pélé people were "a very bad lot," and he was sure there would be no peace on the island until they had been "wiped off." Not only had all his men taken part in the war, but the women also. Tying around them their long aprons, they had painted their faces, and decorated themselves with plumes; then, having gathered all the spare muskets in the village, they had been helping the men in what Manambalea regarded as a holy war!

Was not this sad news for a missionary who had done his utmost to impress upon the people the blessedness of peace? Instruction proceeded among the Tongoans "line upon line, here a little, and there a little"; so Mr. Michelsen was not discouraged, though much distressed by this terrible intelligence. While a true and faithful disciple of the missionary, Manambalea had yet to learn that the Kingdom of God is not extended by violence, but by "righteousness, peace, and joy in the Holy Ghost."

Mr. Michelsen explained that the island was not to be conquered by war, but by Christianity—which is love, and not hatred; life, and not death. Manambalea was soon led to see his error; and, hastening home, he imparted to his people the clearer light which he had himself received. He went further, telling his tribesmen that he intended to go straight up to the bush village, to stop the war. All begged of him to do no

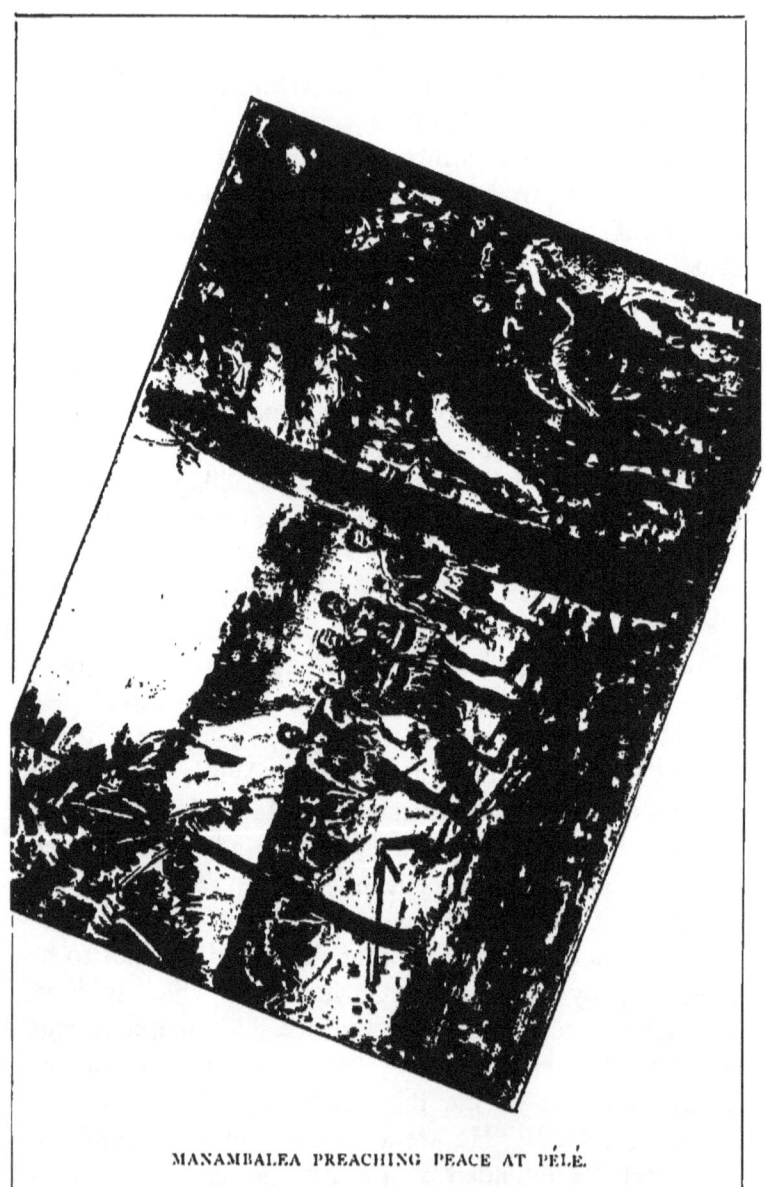

MANAMBALEA PREACHING PEACE AT PÉLÉ.

such wild thing, saying that the people of Pélé would certainly kill him. As he remained firm in his resolution, the villagers proposed to follow him in a body, well armed, so as to afford protection.

This, however, was not Manambalea's wish. He could see that this plan would assuredly mean more war. So, settled in purpose, he went without escort, only taking with him Karisi and another youth. He was, however, followed by his wife and her sister, who declared they would go "and die with him."

The warriors of the bush village could not understand the sight that met their view that day—Manambalea, with whose people they had fought many a battle, coming up to them with two defenceless lads ! There must be some sinister purpose ! The advance of the chief is but part of a plot ! Every fighting-man of Pélé grasped his musket, expecting each moment to see their armed enemy in force. But Manambalea held up his hands, and called, " Stop ! I am not here to fight," he said ; "but to speak peace to you."

At this the men threw their guns to the ground, and stood up, in a respectful attitude, to hear what Manambalea had to say. In a few words he explained that he had been at the mission house, and had related to the missionary what had occurred. " The missionary," he said, "tells me it is not according to ' the Light '* to

---

* This is an expressive designation for the Gospel. Conversely, heathenism is, by native Christians, spoken of as "darkness." Thus : *Natamoli malingo* ("man dark") is used for a heathen ; *sipe malingo* ("ship dark") signifies a Queensland Kanaka cruiser! Could native condemnation of a hateful traffic be more plainly expressed ?

fight and kill people; but that we should love one another and live at peace."

The worthy chieftain further said that he intended to stop fighting; and he hoped the people of Pélé would do the same, and become learners of the "New Doctrine"! Thus what might have been a very disastrous war was brought to an end. Returning to the mission house, Manambalea described what had happened, and suggested that the Gospel should be taken to Pélé on the following Lord's Day—then two days hence. The missionary was, of course, glad to agree to this.

The news of these occurrences spread rapidly over the island; and it is needless to say that many inquired concerning the New Doctrine which had put a stop to war, and led enemies to terms of "peace at all costs." The intention of the missionary to preach at the bush village was also noised abroad, and soon reached Lumbukuti. It greatly enraged Malakaleo: the missionary was actually going to pay a friendly visit to his mortal enemies! Therefore he would "stamp out" the New Doctrine altogether on Tongoa, by killing the missionary and burning down his house!

In the course of the Saturday afternoon the chief of Panita sent for Mr. Michelsen, and said: "Misi, I have heard that you are going to Pélé to-morrow."

"Yes," was the reply.

"I do not think," said the chief, "that you should go; you cannot trust those bush people."

The missionary replied: "They are heathen as well as you, and I have a message for all. I trust in God,

## A Plot to Kill the Missionary.

and consider myself as safe among the bush people as among you."

"Well," rejoined the chief, "if you are determined to go, you should not walk along the ordinary road."

This remark let the missionary into a secret. It was obvious that the chief did not so much fear the harm which the bush tribe might do, as he reckoned upon the intrigue of the Lumbukuti people.

Mr. Michelsen related the facts to his wife, who suggested that perhaps he should not go. His prompt answer was: "Do not be afraid; if there is any danger, the Lord will let us know in due time." Though prepared to flee from village to village, the missionary and his devoted wife determined, with God's help, to remain on the island and continue their Gospel work. They might be harassed, but they would not "emigrate."

Mr. Michelsen continues the story thus :—

"We retired to rest as usual that evening, after having committed ourselves into the hands of God. About one o'clock on Sunday morning, however, there was a knock at the door, and voices were heard outside. I sprang up, and asked what was the matter. Voices said: 'We have come from Selembanga, and want to speak to you.'

"Opening the door, I found some women who had come round the coast on the south side of the island. They informed me that some men from Kurumambe—a village on the north side of the island—had come over and told them that, while at Lumbukuti the previous afternoon, they heard that Malakaleo had ordered nine of his men to go up in the bush and wait on the road where the missionary would pass in going to Pélé, and then kill both him and Manambalea. He had also instructed another company to go over to the mission station, and burn down the premises in the absence of the missionary. What was to be done with Mrs. Michelsen was not disclosed.

"This intelligence showed that Malakaleo had matured his threatened plans to 'stamp out' Christianity; and that the visit to Pélé of myself and the peace-making chief was to open the way. But I at once decided not to take the course which would make the desired occasion. I took the intimations I had received as a message from God; and made up my mind not to go to Pélé as at first agreed.

"After conducting service on Sunday morning at Panita, instead of going on the proposed journey, I returned to the mission house. Subsequently, the band of men whom Malakaleo had instructed to burn down the house, appeared. The leader seemed somewhat taken aback when he found me about the place; and his hand trembled as he held it out to press mine. The band afterwards walked round to where my servant boys were, and there they found Manambalea, a man in whom I never found a trace of timidity or fear. He knew all about the plot, but he spoke quite cheerfully to the men.

"'Oh, you have come!' he remarked.

"'Yes,' they replied; 'we are passing on to the next village to borrow a canoe!'

"Manambalea continued: 'Do not tell us that. Just do what you have come to do!'

"'We have not come to do anything,' said the leader,

hoping to get well and speedily out of his difficult position.

"Again Manambalea taunted them: 'Now just do what you have come to do.'

"'What do you say we have come to do?' asked the Lumbukuti men.

"'Why,' replied Manambalea, glad that this point had been reached, 'to burn down the mission house, of course. We know your designs; now do your work!'

"Having again assured the chief that they had no evil purpose, the men passed on. Instead, however, of going to the village they named, and there borrowing a canoe, they made for the beach, and returned to their own village.

"Malakaleo's evil devices were that day frustrated. Far from 'stamping out' Christianity, his wrath led to measures which resulted in a speedy establishment of the 'New Doctrine' in the hearts of many who would otherwise have continued to thirst after truth and light."

As for "the little Misi"—Karisi—he served for a short time as teacher at Kurumambe, with lasting results attending his work. He had a great thirst for knowledge; was endowed with a remarkable memory; and acquired much facility in the use of the English tongue. In course of time he went to Queensland; and it has recently been reported that he is devoting his energies to mission work among the Kanakas there.

## CHAPTER VII.
## A Flight for Life.

Change of Mission Centre—A Weary March—Arrival on the East Side of the Island—A Gracious Deliverance.

THE time had undoubtedly come for another spot to be selected on which to plant the headquarters of the mission. Not only would the Lumbukuti people not suffer the Gospel to be proclaimed in their own village; they had determined to drive the missionary out of Panita. Night after night the mission house had been eyed by commissioners from Malakaleo ready to shoot at any one that might appear.

Nearly every village in the island was desirous of hearing the missionary's message, and it seemed a great pity to do anything that might unsettle the work. Yet, if Satan's agents were to be foiled, the mission centre must be changed—at least for a time. It was resolved without delay to remove to Manambalea's village, which meant going from the west of the island to the east. Nothing could have pleased Manambalea more than this arrangement. His village was near several others, and it was no rash calculation that, with God's blessing,

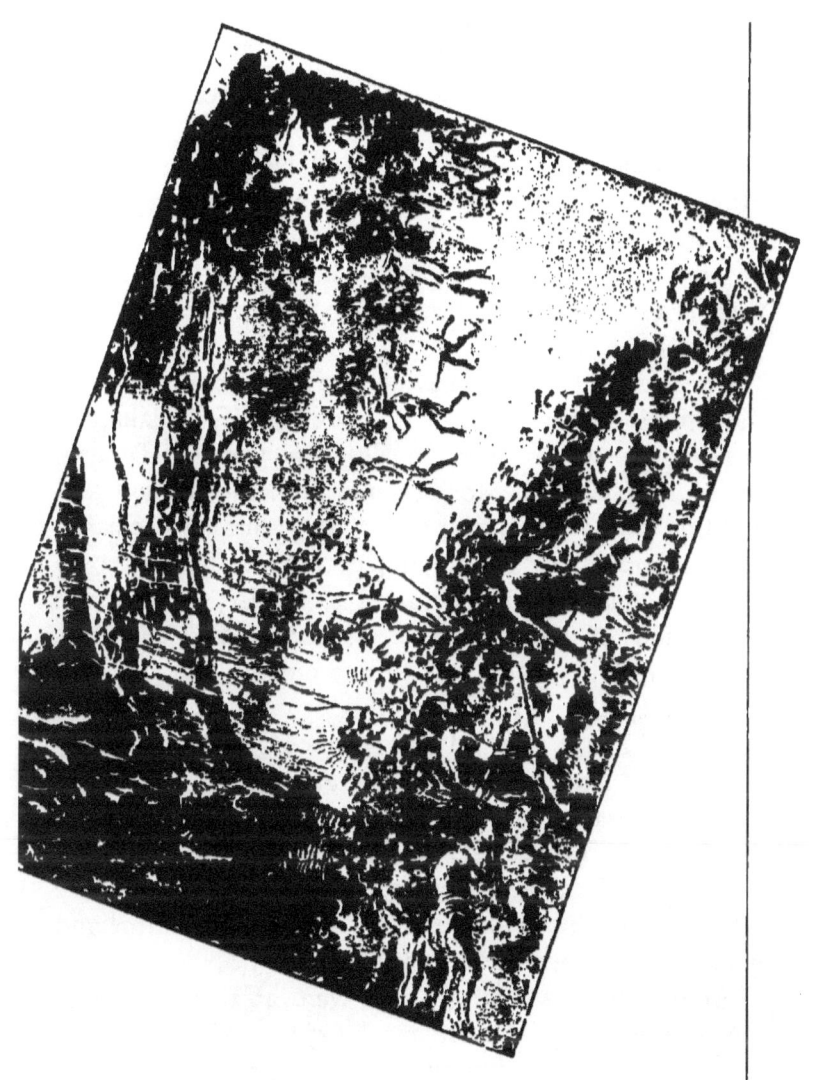

THE WOULD-BE MURDERERS LYING IN WAIT.

the entire side of the island might be reached from that centre.

Manambalea hastened home, and beat the war drum. Having thus called his people together, he explained the situation. His proposal that the missionary should be received at Selembanga was heartily accepted, and there was no delay in forwarding his kindly conceived plans for the removal.

The eventful Sunday having passed without harm to the mission, but to the utter defeat of Malakaleo's designs, a new era began in Christian work on Tongoa. At one o'clock on Monday morning, the women and children of Selembanga arrived at Panita and cleared the mission premises, carrying everything to their own village, which was, they rejoiced to realize, to have the distinction of receiving the missionary and his wife. The men of the tribe also turned out, and stood sentry the while, cheerfully protecting the large body of carriers. There are no conveyances on Tongoa, so everything had to be taken by hand—or by head. Through devious passage-ways, along slippery precipices which would inspire fear in uninitiated pedestrians, the willing people made their way, some carrying unwieldy articles of furniture on their heads, others with arms and hands engaged with goodly loads.

Among the Panita boys who were at this time staying at the mission house, was a nephew of Malakaleo.*

---

* This youth is now chief of Lumbukuti. He stayed for some time at the mission station, and when Mrs. Michelsen arrived on the island, he joined with the native women in the rejoicings already described. In honour of that event he took to himself the name of "Missis." On one occasion he put on a pair of stockings which

With the others, he was shut up during the removal, lest by any means the people of Lumbukuti should prematurely learn what was going on. Altogether, about three hundred natives of Selembanga took part in the removal operations. In the forenoon a band of fighting men from Lumbukuti came up. They were led by their chief, who desired a conversation with the missionary. This was willingly granted.

"Is it true that you are going away?" asked Malakaleo.

"Yes," replied Mr. Michelsen.

"Why?" asked the chief, blandly.

The missionary gave answer, "You have never understood, Malakaleo, why we came to Tongoa. You seem to think that we have come to distribute axes, knives, calicoes, and other things that are desirable for this world's use. We have come here to preach the Gospel, and for nothing else."

Malakaleo: "Do you regard Selembanga as a better place than this?"

Mr. Michelsen: "I do not seek the best place, but people who are willing to hear the Gospel. You do not wish to hear it; the villages on the east side do. Therefore, I go to them. When you wish for the Gospel, let me know; and I will come and give it to you also."

---

the lady missionary had discarded, and otherwise "got up" in his attire, paraded the beach to the amusement of all beholders. The seed of the Gospel was, however, sown in his heart; and later on, while at Queensland, he developed into an active Christian worker (see pp. 138 and 170). His proper name was Timataso, but he is now known by the chieftain's style of Tinabua.

Seeing he could effect nothing by this conversation, the chief addressed Manambalea, showing himself very angry that the latter should "take away the missionary." Manambalea insisted upon the mutual character of the arrangement—the missionary wished to go, and he wished to have him.

The Lumbukuti people having gone away in a rage, the work of removal was proceeded with. Of necessity, this was slow and tedious; and it was Tuesday afternoon before the old quarters were left, to the regret of the chief and people of Panita.

There was neither time nor inclination to travel round the coast to Selembanga, in the footsteps of the carriers. So the journey was made across the island. Manaura,* senior chief of Mangarisu, the good Manambalea, and a young man from his village, escorted Mr. and Mrs. Michelsen, and two youths followed. It was a weary walk through the bush, with all its risks and dangers. Only God could protect them against the murderous bands that infested the region; and into His hands they committed themselves ere ascending the hills. The young man from Selembanga walked cheerfully in front, swinging his gun over his head. He said, "If you hear a shot fired, you will know they have shot me. Then you can run back with all haste."

The party walked on, the silence being broken only by the guides, who talked about the points at which the enemy might fall upon them. Happily, they spoke the Selembanga language, which Mrs. Michelsen did

---

* Manaura was still a heathen; but he was friendly, and open to receive a present for his services. Besides, he was a "sacred" chief, whom no one would dare to hurt.

not understand. In a state of health which quite unfitted her for the fatigue of such a long and heavy walk, her mind was fortunately spared the additional agitation which this conversation would assuredly have caused.

The last two miles of the journey of seven or eight, were "tramped" in utter darkness. When passing through questionable regions, the travellers maintained complete silence. Just before dark, there was a shout by one of those walking ahead. The missionary feared that the enemy had appeared, and his mind was at once occupied with various possibilities and courses of action.

"What is the matter, Manambalea?"

"Oh, we are beyond all danger now." The territory of the Pélé people had been reached, and the Lumbukuti warriors would not venture that far.

Arrived in Selembanga, the missionary and his wife made their temporary home in a grass hut which Manambalea had put up, on land which, some time previously, had been bought for an out-station mission house. They felt much relief in the thought that, humanly speaking, they were "out of danger," in a sense which they had not enjoyed for a long time past.

It afterwards transpired that a band of murderers had been out, lying in wait under a large banyan tree, beside the path! This was passed about twenty minutes before the shout was heard. Why did the savage band not carry out their purpose? The God of Daniel knows—and so do His servants who trust in Him.

## CHAPTER VIII.
## New Mission Quarters.

School Work Advanced—Native Expectations Realized—Sad Fate of a Murderous Band.

HAVING made Selembanga the headquarters of the mission, Mr. Michelsen sought to make his home comfortable and establish evangelistic agencies around him. Houses without floors are a frequent source of fever; so he lost no time in building one more conducive to healthful living. This was made of reed walls and a thatched roof, and had a floor made of boards which were brought from Panita.

In the meantime, material which Dr. J. G. Paton had kindly purchased for Mr. Michelsen arrived from Australia. It was a two-room frame, with an iron roof. The much-needed addition was at once made to the mission buildings. A kind providence timed the despatch of these things, so that the Mission ship did not deliver them at the old station; in which case they might have been a burden during the flight which has been already described.

## Mission House at Selembanga. 73

School work was prosecuted with all possible vigour; and Gospel meetings were held in two parts of Selembanga, and also at Euta, Pélé, and Kurumambe. Yes, indeed, at Pélé, as was promised by Manambalea, when he told its chief that he wished to live at peace with him.

FIRST MISSION HOUSE AT SELEMBANGA.

Even Marimaraki, the chief of Pélé, afterwards showed himself friendly to the mission and to Manambalea; but it was clear that he cared little for the Gospel. He would ring an old cow-bell (stolen in New Caledonia!), to collect the people on Sundays; but he afterwards scolded such as responded to the call and listened to the missionary! The truth seems to be that the old rogue prized the friendship of Mr. Michelsen, in order to keep on good terms with Manambalea, and to be eligible for occasional presents!

After the new house had been built at Selembanga, many of the natives recognised, in the sights that met their eyes, a fulfilment of things that had been spoken

NEW MISSION STATION, SELEMBANGA.

a century or two before, by "a prophet of their own." A long time ago, said the people, before our grandfathers had heard of white men, there was a man among us on Tongoa whose name was Marikitilangi— freely translated: the Son of Heaven. He was not like the rest of the people; even in his youth he never went with the fighting men, but always lived at peace with all.

## A Fulfilment of Prophecy.

That man used to walk about the island, visiting alike the enemies and friends of his village, and speaking kindly to all. Everybody knew him, and no one interfered with him. When he was an old man, and unable to go to the plantation like others, one day he met those who were returning, and said :—

"I have been away to-day. I have seen what shall come to pass many years hence. You shall bury me, and after then these things shall happen: people shall come here who are not like ourselves, but their skin is white. This bark cloth that we use now shall be thrown away, and nice soft cloth that they will give us will be used instead. These stone adzes which we are now using will also be thrown away, and a different kind of tool will be employed. Almost everything shall be changed. Upon the hill there [pointing to the site on which the new mission house had been erected] shall the man live who will show you the Light."

Taking the people down with him to the beach, Marikitilangi pointed out a cave formed by a large flat stone lying against the rocks, and said :—

"Look at this! Our houses are all covered with grass, but the roof of his house shall be like this; it shall be *vatu*"—that is, iron or stone, for one word indicates both in Tongoan.

When the natives who had heard this tradition saw the mission house with an iron roof, standing on the identical hill, they wonderingly said: "This is exactly what Marikitilangi said would be!" When, later on, the missionary made a road from one end of the island to the other, the natives recalled another of the old man's predictions, to the effect that the teacher who would come would "cut the island in two!"

So, as the Gospel was taken from village to village, the people said to the missionary: "This is just what Marikitilangi said you were going to do!" Thus, in a remarkable manner, the natives of the island had been prepared for God's message; and as of old, one had "made straight the way of the Lord."

What appears to be a very important link in the history of the mission was the sad end of Matokae and six of his followers. This man, Malakaleo's "general," was the leader of the band who, with murderous intentions, lay under the banyan tree when the mission party fled from Panita. One day he was winding his way through the bush, past the deserted mission station and the notorious cannibal village of Bongabonga, when, on coming to Meriu, the village of Matabuti, he met Maribatoko (freely translated: Father-leave-him-alone), engaged in building a house.

A quiet laconic man, who seemed to think a great deal ahead of what he said, Maribatoko had stood many a battle with the dreaded Ti-Tongoa, and had shown a firm adherence to principle from the beginning of his Christian life. Matokae asked Maribatoko what he was doing. The reply was, that he was making a *lotu*-house, *i.e.*, a place of worship.

" But you did not ask us about that!"

" No; you are not interested in these things."

" Well, but you should not begin building a *lotu*-house without asking our leave to do so."

" You speak as if we were subject to you; though of you we are quite free, and do as we choose in these

## A Cruel Threat.

matters. Besides, the house is for God, not for you. We know God wishes us to build it, so we have asked no one's permission."

These words were too strong for Matokae, who summed up his indignation with a threat: "You build it, then! We will come and take out one of the sticks, and lash you to it  Then we will carry you home and eat you! We will burn down the house, and that will be an end of it."

The Christian native replied, "You may do as you like; in the meantime the building will go on."

Matokae went to Mangarisu, where he was received with every token of hospitality by Ti-Tongoa. He was invited to remain till the next day; which implied that the chief intended to kill a pig, and make a feast for him. This was according to his gross disposition. After eating and drinking, he lay down to sleep, thinking all was peace and safety. The chief's wife went, during the night, to Marimaraki, her brother, and informed him that his dreaded enemy, Malakaleo's "general," was in their village, and would be going through the bush next morning. Marimaraki's eyes flashed with delight. He speedily called together his fighting-men, to whom he gave information and explicit instructions.

Next morning Matokae made his way through the bush. He carried a large piece of pork, a present from Ti-Tongoa; and two guns, with which to avenge himself on possible enemies. The main object of trust, however, was a "sacred stone," hidden in his belt. When he came near to the banyan tree, where he had, some months previously, awaited the mission party, he was shot dead by the Pélé men, carried off to the village, and eaten. Marimaraki was ready to make any capital he could out of this. So he afterwards remarked to Mr. Michelsen, "Now we have killed Matokae for you." The ready answer was, "I never asked you to do the deed; in fact, I do not at all approve of it."

Further, in order to impress the entire island with a sense of his disapproval of what the chief and his people had done, the missionary, who had been in the habit of visiting Pélé every Sunday, paid no personal visit to the village for a considerable time. Preachers were sent, but the missionary's face was not seen.

It is a remarkable fact that, although several months had elapsed from the time of the flight to Selembanga, and that to be shot in a fight was quite an ordinary thing, no one had been killed on the island from the day of Matokae's murderous expedition until the morning when he himself was shot, and made the subject of a cannibal feast. Not long afterwards three men of the same desperate band were killed and eaten by the bush people. Some time later another three of the band were killed on board a Queensland ship, while attempting to take possession. Only two men of the nine are now alive: one of them is a Church member; the other is, to say the least of it, very friendly to the mission, and there is reason to hope that he will ere long take a decided stand for Christ.

These facts made a profound impression on the people of Lumbukuti; and doubtless had much to do with the friendly attitude of the village at a subsequent period, when the mission centre was again changed.

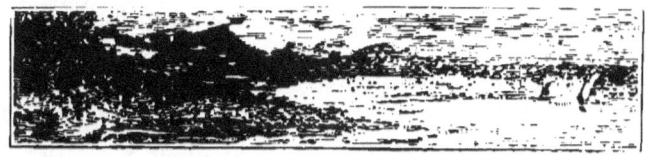

## CHAPTER IX.
## Cannibals Rescued from Cannibals.

Villagers Rescued from the Jaws of Neighbours—Thrilling Incidents, with Remarkable Sequel—A Grand Gospel Triumph.

WHILE the mission house was at Selembanga, a deeply interesting incident occurred, which the missionary shall narrate in his own words:—

At the beginning of 1881 news reached us from Epi that a small village there was being eaten up by a stronger tribe. For generations there had been war between these villages; and at length one of them became so reduced that it was no longer reckoned an enemy, but treated as a prey. Every now and then the stronger village would promote a raid upon the weaker, and capture one or two of the people. These were killed outright, and carried off for a cannibal feast. Thus the smaller village was being gradually exterminated. The circumstances invited prompt action.

I sent over some of our most energetic and enterprising

men, including Manambalea and two of his brothers, telling them to ask the poor people to come and stay with us at Selembanga. Two boat-loads were brought

MARIPAU, ONE OF MANAMBALEA'S BROTHERS.

back, about two-thirds of the remnant, which numbered forty all told.

It was impossible for the boats to touch the rocky shore of Epi. The rescuers had therefore to swim ashore through a rapid current. After inducing the people to accompany them, they returned, being followed through the foaming breakers by the refugees escaping for dear life, some of them with infants on their backs.

The people seemed very much inferior to those of Tongoa, being very thin and haggard. The abdomen was unduly developed, indicating that they had been accustomed to unprofitable food. Fever, early marriage, and consanguineous unions had also left unmistakeable marks on the race.

For the comfort and, if possible, protection of those still remaining, Maripau, one of Manambalea's brothers, was left behind on Epi. Bad weather set in; and for some days the transportation could not be completed. However, it was hoped that all would go well with Maripau and his timid charge—for the most part old women and children. In the meantime, on a Sunday afternoon, Maripau appeared quite unexpectedly at the mission station. The enemies of the people whom he had remained on Epi to look after, had visited, in a body, the partly-deserted village, and called upon him to explain his action. The brave fellow faced them boldly.

"You do not know us," he said; "we are the people of God. Now God loves people, even those whom you are destroying; therefore we have come to take them away, and care for them."

Taken aback somewhat, the leader of the cannibal tribe did not at first manifest much severity. After a few moments he showed by threats the bloodthirsty temper of his party. Maripau's situation was critical. He was not afraid, however. "Full assurance of faith" was one of the graces which he enjoyed. Resuming,

F

he addressed the savage Epians: "Remember, I am God's man. You may shoot me if you like; but if you do, you fight against God."

The spokesman of the tribe remarked: "You say you are God's man, and love men. Why, then, do you carry that gun in your hand?"

This put Maripau somewhat in a difficulty. At length he replied: "We are all accustomed to carrying guns. But you need not suppose that I have any intention of shooting you." With that, he threw the weapon to the ground.

Not much more was said at the time; but Maripau learned from the people whom he was endeavouring to rescue, that the enemy had determined to kill him. Having surveyed the situation, he thought it would be best to make for home, in the hope of hastening the completion of the work of delivering the distressed people. After threading his way through the bush, by unknown paths, a distance of eight miles, he found himself on the south coast of the island. A small canoe lay on the beach; and, praising God for the means of flight (for he could not thank the unknown owner), he made for Tongoa—paddling across a very treacherous current in stormy weather.

Maripau's thrilling story caused much excitement in and around the mission house. The day after he landed, the sea was calmer, and the remainder of the poor people were fetched—Maripau himself accompanying his brother and Manambalea on the expedition.

The refugees were miserably short of clothing; so the first thing that had to be done by their benefactors was

## An Old Chief's Reflection.

to adapt "calico"—which is the common name for all kinds of clothing fabrics—to their immediate needs. The party included an old chief, who, on arriving in the open square, looked around in all directions, and exclaimed: "*Awé, awé!*"—" Dear me, dear me!"

He had been in Selembanga before; and he called to mind that the last visit was about thirty years previously, when he attended a cannibal feast as an invited guest. He was one of those who helped to eat forty Purau men whom the people of Selembanga* had slaughtered. Now, having been rescued from cannibal jaws, he was welcomed with tender compassion by those who had learned a better way of life! Mrs. Michelsen was the first white lady the old chief had seen, and he was so alarmed at the sight that he did not venture to shake hands with her when she cordially greeted him.

The sad experiences of this tribe were evidently overruled by God for the furtherance of the Gospel on Epi. A good while after they had been domiciled in Selembanga, messages were received from their old enemies, asking them to return and live on friendly terms. I refused to consent to any arrangement for a time; but replied that when the refugees were Christians, I would let them go. After the small tribe had passed several years with us at Selembanga, and all were nominally Christian, I acceded to the proposal, on the understanding that a larger tribe should join the smaller under one teacher.

What a grand Gospel triumph is this! No human wisdom was displayed, and no power according to this

---
* See page 120.

world. There was love for Christ and those whom He came to save ; and it proved stronger than the strong one, and those who, under him, were "servants of sin." Need I add that these events made a profound impression upon the people of several villages on Epi. From these I received a number of requests for teachers. They rightly thought that, if Christianity was able to make those who had been enemies for generations to live in peace together, it must be something good, and something which they would also like to have.

Two or three villages on Epi speak the Tongoan language ; the refugee village, however, was not one of them. I had frequently been asked for teachers by the Tongoan-speaking people ; but had none to send. Other missionaries who had some to spare did send.

This part of Epi was for some time under the supervision of Rev. R. M. Fraser, whose station is on the west coast of the island, about thirty miles distant. It was finally arranged by the Mission Synod that it should form part of my district. If I had been in a position to supply teachers at the time I was first asked, the work of God on Epi would doubtless have been much in advance of what it actually is.

## CHAPTER X.
## Another Change of Locale.

The Missionary again Escapes Death—Hindrances Eventuate in the Furtherance of the Gospel.

AFTER labouring for three years mainly on the east side of the island, Mr. Michelsen decided to return to the west. While absent he had sent evangelists every week. It was clear that to reach Lumbukuti and the islands beyond Tongoa, residence on the west coast was necessary. Such a step involved the serious undertaking of cutting a road across the island, from Selembanga to Panita, a distance of six miles, through virgin forest.

The chief of Panita, Maritariliu, whose attitude to the mission was formerly quite friendly, was now an opponent of the work. He had never been in real sympathy with Christianity, but had expected his village to grow in influence through the residence of the missionary. When the mission station was changed to Selembanga, he was disappointed. Hence his present opposition. At this juncture, however, a

"HE RAISED HIS GUN TO FIRE, WHEN MRS. MICHELSEN APPEARED."

[*Page* 88.

kind Providence sent him to Queensland, in a trading vessel, on board which he engaged as boatman. Thus the only difficulty in the way of resumed work at Panita was removed.

This change of locale took place with the warm approval of Manambalea. That unselfish Christian chief assembled his men to transport the necessary mission furniture, and even went with the missionary to reside at Panita until the work was re-established in the west. The resumed operations were attended with signally abundant . blessing. Abandoning their heathen customs, the people readily placed themselves under Christian instruction, and a work of grace was evident in the hearts of many. Everything was inspiring gratitude and hope, when a sudden change came over the scene. Maritariliu returned; and, to his great disappointment, found the people rallying to the missionary, and that his was the only heathen family in the village!

This was too much for him; so without delay he sought to pick a quarrel with the missionary, and harass the people back into heathenism. His wives, whom he had strictly forbidden to have anything to do with Christianity, had. been unfaithful to him during his absence; and as he could say nothing else against the "New Doctrine," he scolded the missionary for not having kept his wives from improper behaviour! Of course, the charge lay at the door of the heathenism to which the chief had bound them.

All day long the chief raved and shouted; and one Sunday morning he sought Mr. Michelsen at a very early hour at the mission station. He reiterated the blame which he had already expressed. It was evidently his purpose to shoot the missionary. He retired to a suitable distance, and raised his gun to fire, when Mrs. Michelsen, who had heard all he said, appeared. This broke the evil spell; and the man, ashamed, lowered his weapon, and went down into the village.

ORIGINAL MISSION BUILDING, WITH ADDITION, AT PANITA.
*(Now removed to Lumbukuti.)*

Following him, by request, Mr. Michelsen witnessed other noisy scenes. The man was undoubtedly " possessed with a devil." He repeatedly said that the devil had told him to kill some one, and that he would assuredly do it. In the midst of the turmoil, people fled from the village, until there were only a few left. For the most part they went to Lumbukuti, the responsible chief of which was now Tinabua, an intelligent and righteous man. After awhile this chief sent Mr. Michelsen a message requesting him not to leave the west side of the island.

The reasonable answer to this was, that it was of no use staying in a village where there were no people. Mr. Michelsen added that, if Tinabua wished the mission station to be on his side of the island, he would need to find accommodation for it in Lumbukuti. This was done, and the land was purchased on which the principal station of the Mission was in due course erected. So, at last, the most suitable place on the island became the headquarters. Malakaleo, the retired chief, saw the Gospel established in the village in which, five years earlier, he refused to allow the missionary to preach; and in which several plots had been hatched against the missionary's life. God overruled all the opposition, and brought to naught the devices of the wicked.

From Lumbukuti the Gospel has spread, not only throughout Tongoa, but to heathen islands in the region. The place is of such commanding importance, and its chief so influential, that villagers far away on the south side of Epi remarked, after Lumbukuti became a Christian village : "When Tinabua puts his foot on our soil we also will become Christian."

## CHAPTER XI.
## Day by Day on Tongoa.

"It is day; let us sing"—First Duties and Breakfast—Morning School—An Accident; the Patient "Baked"—Road-Making at Selembanga—The Missionary's Children and the Native Babies—Sewing-Class Work—Dinner in Comfort and Tea with "Love Apples"—Opening a Mission Box—"Tongoa Toddy"—Translating the Scriptures into Tasiko—Examination of Candidates for Baptism—A Bush School House—How a Church was Built—"Fire! Fire!"—Visitors from Emae—Sabbath Rest and Engagements.

THE missionary thus describes the daily round from the mission centre of Lumbukuti:—

*Toa kokoreko*—"The cock is crowing"; and the songsters of the forest announce the approach of day. No hyenas, no lions, no tigers are there to seek a cool place before the heat of the sun makes life a burden to them. No giant snakes are lying in wait for the early passer-by. Our swarthy island brother has had a refreshing night's rest, and now he stretches himself on his somewhat hard bed of reeds, peeps out of the door, and says to his friends in the house, "*E pei aleati; tunga lega*" ("It is day; let us sing.") The well-known tune of "I am so glad that

## Praise and Prayer.

our Father in heaven," or another equally familiar, is heard from every hut, though the sound is muffled through the grass walls.

After praise and prayer, one and another finds his way out. Among the first are the women, in order to light the fires, whereat to bake a few small yams or breadfruit, whichever may be nearest at hand. Whilst the yam is being baked, the various members of the family are quiet with their books, each studying to fix the daily lesson in his mind, prior to going to school. But even before any one was astir in the other houses, morning devotions were past at the mission station, in the house in which are lodged the young women who stay with us for instruction in life and Godliness. All these girls have had their morning bath, for without this they are not allowed to enter the mission premises. The kitchen lamp having been lighted, a yam or two is peeled and baked in the oven, a breadfruit being also roasted on the open fire. Whilst their business is to prepare our breakfast, these young folk likewise bake something for themselves to take before school. Another girl has skimmed the milk, and is shaking a bottle of cream to make butter for the day; all this before the sun is up.

With the dawn of day one or two more girls come along. They are to sweep the dining-room and set the breakfast-table. In the meantime the cow-herd and the goat-herd appear, each with a billy-can of milk.* The nurse-girl is in the children's bedroom with a tub of water, bathing the little ones. After performing my

---

\* The missionary introduced cows, also goats; and they have fared very well on the island.

own ablutions, I take a hurried look at the passage of Scripture which the natives are to say at morning school, and from which I am to speak. Mrs. Michelsen is soon out setting the cow's milk, and giving the finishing touch to breakfast preparations. The goat's milk has already been strained, and is being heated to make it healthier, and so that it may keep. The entire family is now ready for the morning meal; a reeking plate of porridge, and a jug of cold goat's milk from last night, are ready for us. Also, an abundant supply of yams, two breadfruit, a dish of warmed-up native mushrooms, a native pudding, and a small piece of bread and butter, with a cup of coffee; these make a good and wholesome breakfast, such as we could not get at the best hotel in Europe.

But whilst the children are chatting, King Sol has made his appearance, and the old bell out of the *Madeleine*, which was wrecked on our shore, is jingling. One is often provoked to wish for another and more suitable bell for church and school use; but for all that, there is power in the old bell yet. The second half of the meal is gone through with less ease and comfort than the first. From the impetuous manner in which the boy is ringing, it is getting clear that the school-house is nearly filled, and that he can see no reason why the remaining scholars should not also come along. I hasten down to the school, and so do all the natives on the mission premises, leaving Mrs. Michelsen and the children alone. School over, I go home to attend our morning devotions before the various duties of the day crowd upon us. This morning, however, this quiet season is not to be enjoyed undisturbed.

## "Baking" a Patient.

A man named Pakoa — meaning "Shark," a prænomen as common as the English "John"—has come from one of the bush villages, informing me that a man has met with an accident. Having climbed a tree for a breadfruit for breakfast, he had fallen and sustained some internal injury. "Have they done anything for him?" "Yes; they are baking him." This answer requires some explanation. A long ditch is dug, large enough for the patient to lie down in; a fire is then made in the ditch, a quantity of wood being burnt. Green leaves having been spread over the excavation, the man is laid into it, and thoroughly covered up with foliage and mats. The situation is steaming warm; hence the utility of the treatment. When I came to the place I found the "baking" operation still in progress, and was pleased to hear that the man was improving. I did not disturb him, so long as he was comfortable and doing well. After awhile, however, we took him out. From a careful examination, I concluded that the case was not a very serious one. I gave what further attention I thought necessary, and left, promising to call the next day.

I hurry on to Selembanga, where a large party of men and women are busily working at a road, designed to open up a thoroughfare through Pélé. On my arrival, Manambalea placed himself on a large stone, feeling rather proud of the fact that this obstruction had been effectually rolled off the road. A heathen chief from Tongariki, Samaki by name, stood behind him, smoking his pipe. He was obviously much interested in the road-making enterprise.

Returning home, I find everything going on very much as usual. Our children had been down into the village with some of the native women, to look at the new babies. It had become a very common thing for them to make such visits; and the mothers were pleased, as well as were our little girls. Dinner

ROAD-MAKING ON TONGOA.
*(Heathen Chief from Tongariki looking on.)*

was waiting my return. Our flock of about 100 goats was coming in from the bush; the cows too were in their stalls, looking quiet and satisfied. A number of women were busy on one side of our verandahs sewing their dresses; another crowd of natives waited on the other verandah. These latter had come from Selembanga; but Mrs. Michelsen had been too long with her sewing-class to attend to them. They were cooking a dish of rice, and enjoying the delay. Two members of the sewing-class were also preparing rice. So we sat down to our dinner with feelings of satisfaction that all near and around us had been provided for. One thing, however, was a burden on my mind—the forenoon had passed without my getting any translation work done. So I sent word down to my Tasiko pundits to hold themselves in readiness—to come and help me immediately after dinner. Between the women who had come to sew their dresses, and the Selembanga people desiring to sell their produce, my wife, too, had her hands full. Indeed, she was kept very busy until four o'clock, when the bell rang for her writing-class.

When daylight failed me, I dismissed my pundits, and went out for half an hour's work in our flower garden. When called for tea, I brought with me a handful of love-apples, vulgarly called tomatoes. A dish of boiled pumpkin tops, slightly stewed with a little cocoanut cream, and a beautiful mealy yam, were placed on the table; also home-made bread, home-made butter, and home-made sponge-cake, and a home-made cup of tea—all of them such as can only be got *at home*, and are best enjoyed in the company of one's own dear wife and children. Everything seemed complete; but the love-apples had not been placed on the table. They were soon brought, and then we could wish for nothing more to make up domestic happiness. Blessed is the man who has a happy home! Whilst the table was being cleared, a few pleasant minutes were spent with my two little girls—one on each knee—looking at a picture-book just arrived in a "mission-box" from New Zealand. There being no natives waiting to be attended to, we were able to have worship with our children. Then they were put to bed; and I sat down to refresh myself with a look at *The Christian*—a friend in New Zealand having sent me his copies for an entire year.

The table was cleared, the children were in bed, and native servants were busy over their tea. Another mission-box was opened, for our friends had been very generous this time, and had sent us two. Now is one of those happy hours which only a missionary knows! A flat parcel is taken from the box. It is turned over, and we read, "From Mr. S.'s children—for the children." We spontaneously remark, "Poor things! won't they be pleased to see another lot of picture-books!" Then comes a heavy parcel of printed fabrics. "For the mission-box, with many prayers and best wishes, from Mrs. J. L." Another with similar explanations. Here is a tin. It is pulled out and opened. It contains a well-frosted cake; but on the top of this is a small slip of paper, which is, indeed, to us the most valuable part. On it is written, "To Mrs. Michelsen, with kind love and best wishes, from Mrs. T." And so on. Then we lift something special—a suit of clothes. The inscription is: "For Manambalea, with best wishes, and prayers that he may long be spared to help in the good work." Another parcel—"For Mrs. Michelsen and the children." Tinware, boxes of pocket knives, jews' harps, two large axes, and a few dresses for native women, make up the multitude of gifts from Christian friends. Most of the articles are valuable in themselves; others are of double value on account of the kind words sent with them.

By the time everything is put away, we find it past ten o'clock, and we feel a need for some refreshment. A little water is heated on the kerosene stove, and what has been called "Tongoa Toddy" is made. For the benefit of those who are not abstainers, I may explain how this most invigorating drink is compounded. Take less than half a cup of good goat's milk; one or two heaped teaspoonfuls of oatmeal—real Scotch and fresh; then a little sugar; and—fill up with hot water. Nothing more is required to make a palatable, refreshing, and nourishing drink. Every drinker of this "toddy" will have to find out for himself how much he can take of it, without disturbing his sleep; otherwise, we guarantee—"no headache." While enjoying our "toddy" we go over the mission-box again in conversation, and come to the conclusion that our friends have not forgotten us after all.

The next day begins very much as already described; except that I am not called away, and can go on with my translation work. This goes very well until I come to the words "deliver up" (Matt. x. 21). I look at the Ngunese version; it does not seem to me to be satisfactory. I ask the pundits to give me that in Tasiko. They do so. The result sounds even worse than the Ngunese. Several places where the same word is used are looked up; the idea required to be expressed is carefully explained to the pundits; and they suggest a word which is all that could be wished for one place, but when used in another passage it is found not to suit. A number of words are tried, and

G

one after another is rejected as failing to express the sense adequately. No satisfactory solution of the difficulty is arrived at, so the subject is left till the following day. This is no isolated instance of the difficulties encountered in the work of translating the Scriptures for the islanders. Frequently much time is spent in arriving at a correct rendering of the Inspired Word.

Just at this time my wife informs me that we have nothing for to-morrow's dinner. I hasten to the goat-herd to see if there is a kid suitable for our purpose. The act of killing is performed by a native boy, and I do the more scientific part of the butcher's work. By the time I am ready, tea is waiting.

Arrangements having been made for the baptism of a number of natives, some men and women have called in order to have a private conversation with me during the evening. Tea over, I examined them individually on the fundamental doctrines of sin and salvation; and in most cases received very satisfactory answers. In some instances I found that the replies to certain questions had been "got off" between the candidates. I therefore put my questions in unexpected terms; but as a rule, after the examination, I formed opinions very similar to those of the native teachers, who had a more particular knowledge of the individual character and life. The whole evening is thus occupied; my wife being engaged in putting the children to bed, setting the bread, and writing letters to friends far away.

The next morning I have to make an unusually early start—to be up at one of the bush villages in time for school. I arrive shortly after the proceedings have

## A Bush School House. 99

opened; and, some time before reaching the place, I hear a shrill voice saying "*ba*," and a deep bass voice repeating the word. Then I hear "*be*," then "*bi*," then "*bo*," and so on. More or less throughout the school similar spelling exercises are in progress; and the attendants, as usual, range from the oldest man to the youngest

BUSH SCHOOL HOUSE, EUTA, TONGOA.

child. School is opened and closed with singing and prayer.

On looking round, I find that some of the "pupils" are repeating portions of Scripture; there are among them aged folk who can quote several long passages of the Word of God, which they have learned by this process, although unable themselves to read a single word. To find things proceeding in this rough and ready, somewhat scampish, way, did not surprise me; for the natives have continually to be checked in their teaching operations, which appeal excessively to the ear, and too little to the eye. Gaining attention, I give the school a short lecture on the art of teaching and learning. Routine work being continued, there is half an hour's reading. After this I examine them in a simple Scripture catechism. Here they do better; every one can answer the questions perfectly — by whatever means they had learnt the subject. Subsequently I give an address of about a quarter of an hour, specially dealing with the answers that have been given during the catechizing. After school there is more or less of a feeling for some additional reading, so several of the scholars sit down outside the building for this purpose.

Less than an hour's walk brings me to Selembanga, where four or five natives are waiting for me. The erection of a new church is no small undertaking, and for a long time preparations had been in hand. The material — Australian hard wood — had been got from Sydney, whilst the rafters were of Norwegian fir. The native assistants had shown themselves quite expert with saw, chisel, and hammer, and to-day the whole village was called together for the crowning event. The side walls — sixty feet long by twelve feet high — were, to the great astonishment even of those who did the deed, lifted bodily and placed in position; and then, amid rejoicings, the ends were raised and fastened, making the building thirty-three feet wide. Thus the edifice was reared in one day. I returned in the evening, about eight o'clock, perhaps feeling, no less than the people of Selembanga, that a good day's work had been done.

I was hoping, after a late tea, to spend the remainder of the evening quietly. About 9.30, however, we were startled by calls from the distance. I went out on the verandah to hear what it was, and distinguished voices on the sea calling out "*Nakápu! nakápu!*" (Fire! fire!) It was a boat from Emae, with a little company on board who had been rowing for hours against a strong current, and were wanting to see the landing-place; hence their call for a light. The people of the village, as well as some from the mission station, have heard the call, and fire brands are speedily seen moving from all quarters down towards the beach.

The boat is soon ashore, and the Tongoans give the visitors a hearty welcome, assisting them in every way possible. The luggage includes baskets of shells, brought to the mission station for sale, and baskets of yam to serve as presents to friends. Ascertaining the fact that visitors had come, we ordered that a pot of rice should be cooked. In due course the strangers reached the mission station, which is about three-quarters of a mile from the shore. Men and women came into the house to press our hands, and then we learned the character of their principal business. A couple wished to be married, and as Emae was under my charge during the absence of Rev. Peter Milne in New Zealand, it was desired that I should tie the knot. After supper, a teacher and a few others from Emae engaged us in conversation regarding the work of God. It was near midnight when we retired to rest, happy in the thought that the Emae party was hospitably entertained.

The week's work being ended, the much-needed Day of Rest has come. Whilst firmly believing in *all* the Ten Commandments as the unalterable law of God for the life of man on earth, I have always endeavoured to make the sweet memorial of our Lord's Resurrection to dawn upon the Tongoans as a holy privilege for the people of God, rather than as a stern ordinance from the Judge of all the earth. This latter aspect cannot, of course, be entirely overlooked ; and it must be made clear to the people that we are *commanded* to keep the day holy. It has been our wont to observe the day in the way that would be most glorifying to God, and most for the spiritual benefit of the people. We do not by any means lay down a strict rule about taking nothing but cold food, nor how much is to be cooked ; but we teach them to do as little work as is consistent with health and a fair amount of comfort. The result, I feel sure, is that the day is bright and happy, and that the enjoyment of it is more in the sweetness of holy exercises than in mere rest and exemption from work.

There being no school on the Lord's Day, the people rest a little longer than usual. At sunrise a few small yams or breadfruits are soon baked, which make the principal part of the breakfast. Besides this, we always give all who are staying on the station a cup of tea and a piece of bread, so as to reduce their cooking to a minimum. In every hut is heard the voice of song and praise. Then one may see some reading, and others getting themselves dressed for church. At

## A Sabbath Day's Preaching Tour.

nine o'clock the churches are filled with worshippers. The service lasts about an hour and a half, and afterwards the people gather themselves into small groups in various houses, and have a hymn and prayer. That over, a good while is spent reading the Word of God. While my wife returns to the station with the children, to give them some instruction, a few of the natives—perhaps some five or six—gather round me, and follow me on my preaching tour round the island. This, of course, is a most interesting, though very fatiguing, work. I have no fixed plan for this tour. I consider the weather, my own strength, and the need of the villages.

As a rule, I return to my station some time after dark, having walked and preached continuously from nine o'clock in the morning. Whatever the day has been to others on the island, it has been no day of rest to me. Tea is waiting; but I cannot take it. Two or three sips must suffice; and, after twenty minutes' rest and a warm bath, I am revived, and able to join my family at the table.

Whilst the day has been thus with me, some of the native teachers have been moving about on similar errands, and other converts have been rendering such assistance as lies within their power. At the mission station, in the afternoon, there is Sabbath-school, and, in the evening, a native teacher conducts public worship in the church.

## CHAPTER XII.
## An Unexpected Cloud.

Jane Langmuir—Parentage and Training—Missionary's Wife and Helpmeet—Devotion to the Mission—"I am so Unworthy!"—Departure "to be with Christ."

MENTION has already been made in a note on page 57 of the sad bereavement which has quite recently befallen Mr. Michelsen. The deceased lady was a true helpmeet in the work on Tongoa, and this story of perils and triumphs must of necessity include a sketch of her life from the pen of her bereaved husband :—

My beloved wife was the daughter of John Langmuir, who was the son of a farmer near Paisley. Having learned the business of a gardener and florist, and married an Irish lady, he went to Australia about 1838. For many years they lived near Melbourne, and had a large family, whom they nurtured in the fear of God. After about twenty years' residence in Victoria, they removed to New Zealand, in order that their youngest daughter, Jane, might have the benefit of a more bracing climate. They settled near Dunedin, and the change was beneficial in the sense desired.

## The Late Mrs. Michelsen.

In Scotland John Langmuir had been connected with the Established Church; in New Zealand he became connected with Christians known as "Brethren"; whilst his children attended the Presbyterian Sabbath School, and some of them became teachers there. In 1877 he

THE LATE MRS. MICHELSEN, WITH THIRD CHILD.

passed to his rest, aged about 66, leaving a widow and six children—three sons and three daughters—to lament their loss. Some of these had already left home, and others were soon to do so. At length, Jane alone remained to sweeten the home of the lonely widow.

I had seen her often with her father at the Depôt of

the New Zealand Bible, Tract, and Book Society, at Dunedin. She was rather slender, and looked exceptionally thoughtful for her age—then a girl of seventeen. I cannot say that I thought then that she would become my wife. But no one could help noticing one of her age enjoying so much the company of Christians of mature experience. A word I once heard from a young lady friend and companion of hers, did much to awaken my interest in Jane. I said, "Those Langmuirs seem very nice Christian people." "Yes," she said, "and particularly the youngest."

In 1878 I left New Zealand for the mission-field. After spending a year on Nguna, I went to Tongoa to commence a mission by myself. A lonely European among a thousand savages, I could not remain alone. Indeed, a very unpoetic resolution was passed by the Synod in Otago, that I should take a trip up to the colonies to be married and ordained! The second of these could easily be done, and I felt confident that the Lord would help me also regarding the other. There was no lack of friends who were ready to give me advice and help if needed. My mind was directed to the sweet Christian girl I had seen every day on her way to the High School in Dunedin, and who had often visited the Book Society's sale room. I laid my proposal before her. She had two difficulties—one was that she did not think she was fit for such a work; and the other, that she thought of her duties to her aged mother, who had no one else with her. She said nothing about the cannibals; an objection which I might well have expected, as she had a few days previously been present at a meeting at which I

## Prepared to go.

had given harrowing accounts of cannibalism. Indeed, some candid friends had cautioned me: "If you wish to find a wife, you had better not say anything about the cannibals." My argument was, that I wanted a wife who would be prepared to meet anything for Jesus.

When I saw her again, she said she was prepared to go if her mother was agreeable; but she felt it her duty to submit to her mother in this matter, as it meant leaving her alone. I shall never forget the moment when her dear old mother gave me her reply. With trembling voice she explained to me how that Jennie had been her only comfort in widowhood—now about thirteen years—and that, more than ever, she needed some one with her. It was not a question with her whether her daughter would make a good match or not. The case stood before her mind thus:—The Lord had asked for her, and although she had no one dearer on earth, she could not keep her from Him. She knew quite well that she would go away to live among the South Sea cannibals, of which the people of the colonies had heard so much; so that an account of her daughter being devoured by them would be no surprise.

After the dear old lady had given her consent, I felt exceedingly unhappy about taking her daughter from her. The weeks soon passed away, however, and I have no doubt they seemed too short altogether for the poor mother. When she stood on the wharf to bid us farewell, and felt that she could do no more for the child for whom great sacrifices had been made, and who, in turn, had been such a comfort to her, she called after me between her sobs and tears: "Take care of my daughter." I tried to smile as kindly as I could, and told her that her guarantee was that she was now *my wife*. I do not think she knew what I said, but I heard her say: "Yes, *you* may smile . . ." When others had left the wharf, she remained to lift up her feeble arm, to wave her handkerchief to the daughter whom she scarcely expected to see again.

My young wife landed on Tongoa amid the stormy rejoicings of the native women. Natives came from all parts of the island to see the lady missionary, and even Malakaleo seemed quite moved when listening to her playing on the organ. The chilly, unhomely house was soon turned into a happy home. Cleanliness, order, and brightness, became impressive elements in the new order of things. When returning from a fatiguing tour over the island there was a warm bath, a tidy table, a well-cooked meal, and a loving reception—a very different state of things from that which obtained a year before. I was often calling to mind some words of Rev. Dr. Inglis before I left Dunedin: "You need not think of working in the New Hebrides without a wife. Many will remind you that you should find a lady with a teacher's certificate, and all that sort of thing. My advice is: 'Get a good wife.' You will have to do most of the teaching; but a good wife will make your life easier, and thus enable you to do more work. She will also save you from an endless variety of trivial things which you otherwise would have to do."

Months and years were made bright and happy, and the wisdom of the worthy Doctor's remarks abundantly verified. Not that she was deficient in the art of teaching, nor that she did not do it. She did much in this direction, and also instructed the women in

"Her Presence saved my Life!"

sewing and housekeeping; she was an excellent housekeeper and cook. But her help to me lay mainly in making home comfortable and happy, and in being a true and wise companion and counsellor.

This beloved helpmeet has now been taken from me; therefore I can speak with freedom of her worth. In all possible ways she shared my responsibilities and anxieties. She carried on a Sabbath School, as it might be called—a class for the young. To her disappointment, at first, she found that several of the better instructed young men of the village attended. Feeling that they received useful instruction, they continued to come, and in increasing numbers. She was almost invariably with me on my voyages from island to island; and if ever she thought I might be in danger, she insisted on being with me. When a savage lifted his gun at me to fire, she appeared on the scene; as she afterwards said, she thought it was time for her to come out too. Her presence saved my life.

As a doctor she was an important acquisition to the mission. She had little faith in what generally passes for orthodox physic; in difficult cases she generally consulted all the books within reach, and then took the course which commended itself to her own judgment. Though I was supposed to be the doctor, I always had a private consultation with her before treating any case involving special care.

She loved singing, but had not a strong voice. Two of her favourite hymns were those beginning:

"At the feet of Jesus, listening to His word;"
and
"When peace like a river attendeth my way."

## An Unexpected Cloud.

It was in London, on December 30th, 1892, that she was called home. She had given birth to a little boy, and was hoping to recover her usual strength; but fever supervened, and in a few days her course on earth was finished. She had almost a painful sense of her own unworthiness. The day before she died, she asked my pardon that she, who was so unworthy and unfit, had had the presumption to go with me to the mission-field. It was her earnest desire and prayer that the Lord would give her another opportunity to serve Him more faithfully than she had done. I reminded her of the perfect goodness and the love of God, whereupon she exclaimed, "Yes, He is so good—so good!" but with a tone which implied what she so often had said, "and I am so unworthy." She loved the work with her whole soul, and while on furlough often remarked: "I wish we were home again on Tongoa."

When I told her not to be troubled about her four little ones, as I was sure the Lord would care for them, she said, "I am not the least troubled about them; I *know* He will care for them." Again, when I asked her to forgive me any unkind word I might have said to her at any time, she replied, "Yes—everything"; and added in an energetic voice, "*God bless you!*"

Towards the end of her pilgrimage, she often sang, with much feeling :—

"Master, the tempest is raging!
The billows are tossing high."

When she felt the surging billows of Jordan around her, I read the hymn to her. On coming to the chorus:

"The winds and the waves shall obey My will,
*Peace! be still!*"

## Last Moments.

her soul seemed as if it were on the other side already. She exclaimed in a strange and distant voice, "Yes; oh yes!" Though naturally rather timid, it may be testified of her that she lived out the counsel of the lines :

> "Where duty calls or danger,
> Be never wanting there."

Her mother had the joy of seeing Jennie just once after first bidding her farewell. That was in 1884. She was hoping soon to embrace her again; but has survived to hear of her daughter's departure " to be with Christ." For each and all of us there is the consolation : " Neither death nor life...shall be able to separate us from the love of God, which is in Christ Jesus our Lord."

## CHAPTER XIII.
## Cannibalism and its Horrors.
### The Motives of Cannibalism—Deeds of Horror, and Tales of Woe.

THE horrors of cannibalism cannot be realized by written descriptions. Mr. Michelsen's missionary career from the first has been in the midst of people sunk to this depth of degradation.

What is the motive of cannibalism? Unquestionably the depraved appetite of fallen man, in his lowest estate, is gratified by the taste of human flesh. The chief of Pélé, an island near Nguna, once remarked: "Pig's flesh is bad, and human flesh is good." This is a declaration of the comparative excellence of the latter as estimated by the cannibals themselves.

Another motive is a wish to show how entirely they can vanquish their enemies: they make food of them! Malakaleo, the chief, who was so bitterly opposed to the Gospel at first, answered a message from his enemies with the threat—"We will eat you!" In the old days

## A Fearful Murder.

there were no feasts so high as those at which human flesh was partaken of.*

One day, while Mr. Michelsen was helping Mr. Milne on Nguna, news arrived of a fearful murder having been committed on the island of Efate, the other side of Nguna Bay. The two missionaries repaired to the spot, and ascertained the facts. A number of natives from the island of Makura had arrived in Efate, just opposite Nguna, to dig some *taumako*, a vegetable similar in appearance to the potato. The chief who instigated and led in the murder, had been among Europeans, in Queensland and elsewhere, for thirteen years, and could speak English well! He denied having killed any one; but while the words were in his mouth, evidences of his guilt were forthcoming. In the surf on the beach lay the trunk of a human body; in a canoe alongside was the head; and the arms and legs were roasting on a fire in the neighbouring village.

Confronted with proofs of his crime, the brutal fellow readily excused himself. The things said by the missionaries were quite right and good for the white man, but they do not suit the black man! Accompanying the missionaries was Matakoale, a Christian chief from Nguna. Stepping forward at this juncture, and laying

---

* Next in honour as food came the pig, which is to-day held in high esteem on the island. Pigs and fowls (and no other animals) multiply in every village. When a man bought a wife in the old days, he would pay for her in so many pigs—ten or fifteen, according to assessed value. It was customary to sacrifice both classes of animals to the spirits. Pigs so devoted were killed by a knock on the head, and not by being bled. When Christianity began to make head-way, the question came into vogue—" Is the pig bled or not?" If bled, there was no heathenism about it.

H

his hand on his breast, this man said: "I am a black man, and I know that Christianity suits me."

Seeing they could accomplish nothing, the missionaries left for the mission station in the boat which had conveyed them across the bay. When a short distance out from land, they saw a procession along the beach. The body of a man, lashed to a stick, was being carried by two persons. A shell* was blown, and some young men went in front, swinging spears over their heads. This was in bravado of the act of murder. Others followed, filled with the same evil spirit. When the true facts came to light, the worst fears were realized; for several persons had been killed, and the bodies were sent as presents to friends!

The crime was excused by the statement that, some time previously, a number of natives of Epi, working for a planter on Efate, had stolen his boat, in order to make their way home. While passing Makura, they were induced by the natives to go ashore, and forthwith were murdered and eaten. The chief of Makura, on whose order this horrid deed was committed, was the man whose mutilated body the missionaries found in the surf at Efate, as just described. Thus the act was one of revenge. It was also explained that the Makura men on a previous visit had taken some earth with them from Efate, and by means of it, *i.e.*, by incantation, had caused a drought from which the islands were then suffering!

---

* A conch shell. Sometimes these are about a foot in length—two shells being joined together. They are capable of producing an alarming roar.

## CHAPTER XIV.
### Three Tongoan Martyrs.

Not "Moved Away"—Manoai's Firmness—A Bush Tragedy—
The Last Cannibal Feast.

SHORTLY after the second break-up of the Panita station, it became necessary for Mr. and Mrs. Michelsen to take a trip to New Zealand. No sooner had they left the island, than the chief of Panita caused one of his men, who would not be removed away from the faith of the Gospel, to be shot. That man, though simple and uninfluential, was the first martyr in the island.

The second witness unto blood was also shot during the missionary's absence. There was an elderly man at Selembanga, named Manoai, a decided and earnest Christian. He was too old to be sent out as a teacher; when, however, he heard of the missionary's intention to leave the island for a time, he asked what he could do to advance the work. He was glad to receive instructions to visit the refugee Epians daily, to see that they attended school, and otherwise to exercise an influence for Christ among them. This charge he kept faithfully so long as he lived.

He did not live long, however. One of the bitterest enemies of the Gospel in the village was a man with whom, as a heathen, Manoai was formerly on friendly terms. This man, hating the light, conceived a hatred for his former friend; and meeting him one morning in the road, inquired where he was going. Manoai's answer was, that he was about to visit the Epians. His enemy knew the religious object of the visit, and at once declared his intention to shoot his Christian neighbour.

"You may do as you like about that," said Manoai. "You can kill my body, but you cannot do any more; my soul shall go to heaven." Manoai stood still, looking his opponent in the face. The murderous threat was at once put into execution!

The third martyr sealed his life-testimony about five years ago, under singular circumstances. Many years previously, when the village of Pélé was at war with another, one of the wives of the chief fled to Kurumambe, her native place. She had her infant boy with her. After the war, the chief insisted upon his wife's return; and she went back, leaving her boy at Kurumambe. As he grew up, he was in the habit of visiting Pélé, where he had free access, as the then ruling chief, Marimaraki, was his half-brother.

The young man's name was Bulilio, and in the course of time he confessed Christ. Of an earnest disposition, whenever he went to Pélé, he preached the Gospel to his kinsmen and others. This gave great annoyance to the chief, who at length decided to put an end to it.

He instructed his men to shoot him; and this was done as he was passing through the bush from the village. The young man ran some distance, and then fell. It was thought that he had escaped; but some days later the body was found in a state of decomposition.

What followed shows the ferocity of Marimaraki. When the corpse was conveyed into Pélé, the people said: "Let us not eat this man; he is one of our own—brother of the chief." The chief himself replied, "If you will not eat him, I shall."

Not having the moral courage to insist upon burial, the people assented to the proposal. Mr. and Mrs. Michelsen, at Lumbukuti, saw the smoke of the enormous fire which was kindled for the purpose of roasting the corpse.

*This was the last martyr on Tongoa for the faith of Christ. And it was the last cannibal feast on the island!*

## CHAPTER XV.
## Native Superstitions: A Religion of Dread.

Native Acknowledgment of the Creator — "Sacred" Men — *Kaimasi*, or Witchcraft — Other Cruel Customs — Fear of "Deceiving Spirits."

O far as they are capable of being grouped together, the superstitions of Tongoa make up a system of fear. It was held to be necessary continually to appease the wrath of the "spirits."

Tongoan superstitions, for just twice in the year, acknowledged an omnipotent Creator. In the times of planting (about October–November) prayer was offered for His blessing; and at the gathering of the first-fruits (about February) thanks were offered to Him for His bounty. Doubtless the spirits were recognised here also; but yet the truth remains that, with all their darkness and ignorance, the Tongoans admitted the witness of God, that He "gave rain from heaven and fruitful seasons, filling our hearts with food and gladness" (Acts xiv. 17).

## "I am only Joking."

Every village had its sacred man, who was sometimes a chief. He undertook many functions: sacrificing to the spirits, to avert their anger, on behalf of sick persons; and practising *Kaimasi* (a kind of witchcraft), to compass the evil, or bring about the death, of obnoxious individuals. Sometimes these occupations were in very skilful hands. Cases of sacred women are less common. One at the village of Fila, on Efate, was so powerful that she kept Christianity back several years by her enchantments.

Samori, the chief of Voitasi, a small village on Tongoa, was the representative of a once influential family, which also held chieftainship on Emae. Amongst sacred chiefs, his position was so high that he was called "the Son of God." Addressing him on the subject of Christianity, Mr. Michelsen reminded him that, being "the Son of God," he ought to be the foremost to accept the Gospel! When the man showed a procrastinating disposition, he was asked whether, in case he were living away from home, a letter from his father would not secure his utmost attention. He replied in the affirmative; whereupon Mr. Michelsen told him that he was the bearer of a message from God. Feeling the force of the argument, the chief replied, with regard to his pretensions: "I am only joking." If he had maintained his claims, he would have felt compelled either to accept or to reject the message brought by the missionary.

The practice of *Kaimasi*, which is similar to the *Nahak* of Tanna, is essentially witchcraft, and is very mischievous. It is believed that, by becoming possessed of remnants of what a man has eaten, or of anything that has come from him, his death may be caused When the sacred man buries the remnant or morsel, the unsuspecting man's death-warrant is sealed! Therefore, if a native sucks sugar-cane, he is careful to retain the fibre for destruction when he gets home. Again, if a native is away from his own village, and eats bananas, he takes home all he does not consume, so as not to come under the power of actual or possible enemies. Thus, in many circles, fear and revenge become the warp and woof of social life.

Death from a natural cause was no part of the creed of Tongoa before the missionary gave the people the Gospel. If a man died, some one had caused his death—that was at once fact and argument. Aged believers to-day relate many illustrative occurrences. Here is one :—

About thirty years ago, the chief of Selembanga died, probably of consumption. After consultation with soothsayers, it was "ascertained" that the death had been caused by the people of Purau, another village. Of course the act must be avenged! After the days of mourning—probably a hundred days—the people of Purau were invited to attend a feast at Selembanga. Nothing suspecting, they went, and a carousal followed. In the middle of the night, while engaged in a dance of the vile character usual on such occasions, the people of Purau were suddenly set upon by their treacherous "friends." About forty men were slain.

Cannibal feasts were afterwards held, bodies being sent in all directions to acquaintances and friends of the murderers. Moreover, the people of a village on the island of Epi, to the north, were invited over to Selembanga to help to eat the victims of the massacre.*

The chief Malakaleo had an only daughter, whom he loved dearly. She sickened and died. To show his affection for her, he ordered that two of his wives should be buried alive in her grave. Thus the departed one would have, in the spirit-world, companions who would attend to her requirements. The poor women appealed in vain to the chief; he was deaf to all entreaties for mercy, as also were other men of influence who were visiting at the house of mourning. Malakaleo himself struck them with clubs, and drove them into the grave; and thus his decision was carried into effect.

Though the savage heart was not touched by the cries of his sacrificed wives, Malakaleo's conscience was not at ease after the terrible event. He always imagined that their spirits were about the place, and that they threw stones into the house at night. So, regularly, at the close of the day, he hung a basket of food outside, for them to partake of should they desire! Even then the miserable man was haunted with the notion that his wives were avenging his cruelty. So he ordered his other wives to fence off the house in which they were buried; for, as is often the case, the grave was in one of the family houses. The incident shows that in dark Tongoa, with all its brutality, there was a real bondage arising from fear of death and dread of the dead.

* To this very feast came the old Epian chief who was afterwards, with his people, rescued from cannibals, as related in Chapter IX. (page 79).

## 122 Native Superstitions: A Religion of Dread.

The story has already been told of some families who were rescued from cannibals on the island of Epi, and cared for at the Selembanga station. The son of the chief, the object of all the family hopes, died. Though he owed his life to Christians on Tongoa, the old man was not at the time so weaned from the cruelties of native superstition as to have mercy upon his wife. According to custom, he determined that she should be buried with the boy.

Mr. Michelsen describes what followed :—

"I entered the house just as the old man was getting hold of his gun. When I took that weapon from him, he seized an axe, hoping to do his heartless work therewith. I took the axe also out of his hands. He raved with anger; and while I reasoned with him, he put his fingers in his ears. As he would listen to no argument, and was deaf to all appeal, I sent for some Christian natives, and instructed them to take the wife under their protection until the youth had been buried. This was done, and the woman's life was saved."

Here is another tale of cruelty :—

The chief Tarisaliu, of Purau, and his people, notorious as thieves and ruffians, incurred the displeasure of nearly every tribe on the island. Settling near Lumbukuti, and placing himself under the protection of the chief, he sought to cement the subsisting friendship by a horrid deed. One day, out walking, he saw in front of him an old woman belonging to his own village. He took his gun and shot her dead, sending her body to the chief as an expression of his affection!

"Laying the spirits" was a serious matter. On a report that spirits had been seen about, there was nothing to be done but to discharge a goodly quantity of gunpowder in the locality. Whether as an act of defiance towards the spirits, or as a menace to more substantial intruders, this measure had the reputation of being eminently satisfactory. The trust of the natives was, in a very emphatic sense, in the gun; although they all grieved at times over its ravages in their family circles.

In the following incident the missionary illustrates the popular fear of " spirits ":—

"One evening, during the year spent on Nguna, I had been over to Efate with three natives. Just as we came out of the narrow boat passage at Havannah Harbour on to Nguna Bay, we saw a squall coming up from the west. We hoped to be across the Bay before this would reach us; and as the sun was just setting, we could not afford to wait. The squall overtook us, however, much sooner than we anticipated; a heavy sea came in, and darkness enveloped us.

"The boat was fast being filled—it was only a small craft that two men could easily carry—and we committed ourselves to Him who holds the waters in the hollow of His hand. The sea and wind grew in strength, until one of the natives was so paralysed with fear that I was compelled to take his oar, and ask him to steer. This arrangement had not long been made when the man who was steering saw a light on Nguna. This would certainly have guided us to the coast, although it might also have led us into a strong and dangerous current which ran along the shore. The man, however, directed the boat away from the light, which he concluded was a manifestation from 'deceiving spirits.' We rowed for hours, not knowing where we were.

"About twelve or one o'clock we heard breakers, and I moderated the rowing, lest we should be swallowed up. When able to see more clearly, I recognised the outline of Efate near the point from which we had started! We followed the land, and before we knew of it, we found ourselves in a great calm. We were back in the boat passage from which we had started some six hours previously!

"Then I learned how it was we had toiled in vain; for the superstitious man took credit for not being misled by the 'deceiving spirits.' Moreover, I was satisfied that his ignorance had been overruled to the saving of our lives; for, if we had attempted to land at Nguna in such a sea, we might have been drowned by the swamping of the boat."

## CHAPTER XVI.
## Two Wrecks: a Contrast.

The First: attended with Plunder and Cannibal Designs—The Second: the Occasion of Kindly Hospitality.

A YEAR or so after the mission station was established at Selembanga, the Queensland labour trader *Chance* sailed round Tongoa, and her boats called at the village. A young man who was a servant at the mission house went on board with the intention of going to Queensland. The missionary despatched a note to the captain, requesting him to send the lad back. He added the words: "If the boy is not *sent* back, I will see to it that he *comes* back." The meaning was not obvious; but Mr. Michelsen was mindful of the fact that it was contrary to the provisions of the Queensland Labour Act to remove a white man's servant.

The message vexed the captain very much, and he sent the young man ashore; but at the same time made strenuous efforts to carry off several scholars of the Mission. In this he succeeded. Exceedingly grieved, the missionary prayed the Lord yet to send back the youths that were thus going beyond his reach. In conversation with some of the natives, he told them what he thought of the Queensland traffic; and added: "If some should insist upon going, do not go in the *Chance*; because I know she is a dangerous vessel, and will go down some day. It has, in fact, been reported to me that her plates are as thin as a sixpence!"

There the matter was left; and Mr. Michelsen hardly expected to hear more of it. The next day, to his surprise, he saw one of the scholars whose departure he had begun to lament approaching the mission station. Inquiring, "Are you paid off already?" he was answered: "Yes; and we paid ourselves!" The youth then explained that the ship had gone on the rocks near the heathen village of Mangarisu; but that the people there had stopped them from proceeding earlier to the station, as they were plundering the ship, and did not wish the missionary to interfere.

Accompanied by Manambalea, Mr. Michelsen at once walked over to Mangarisu. Before they got down to the beach, they met a number of natives carrying bundles of axes, cases of tobacco, rolls of calico, tins of preserved meat, gin, gunpowder, and other commodities of "civilization." Questioned respecting their conduct, they paid little attention; they had made great hauls, and were excited and beyond control.

The captain and ship's crew—some of them under the influence of intoxicants—walked up to Meriu, where there was a schoolhouse, in which they sought refuge. Meanwhile, the Mangarisu men were engaged in a consultation about slaying and eating the strangers. As many of the white men as were sufficiently sober to walk, accepted hospitality at the mission station, and the others were given into the care of trustworthy men.

So the island was spared what might have proved a cannibal feast of a specially tragic type. One of the sailors explained that, as fast as the goods were conveyed ashore, the people carried them off.

The agent of the Queensland Government, an exceptionally refined man, sailing in the *Chance*, transferred the fire-arms to a boat, and brought them to Selembanga. Many of the villagers were little more than heathen at the time, and they thought this a splendid opportunity to help themselves. Mrs. Michelsen, having seen the boat, appeared on the scene just in time; ordered the restoration of every piece that had been handled; and organized a band of women who carried the fire-arms up to the mission station.

Ultimately the shipwrecked company was taken away by another vessel, and landed safely at Queensland.

Another wreck-scene on the island is altogether different. About five years later, in 1888, while the head-quarters were at Lumbukuti, the Queensland ship *Madeleine* left her moorings, and was blown ashore in a hurricane. The contents were safely lodged in Mr. Michelsen's boat-house, the natives rendering all the help in their power. The captain proceeded in a boat to the island of Malekula, and invited other ships to attend an auction sale on the beach at Lumbukuti. This was held, and everything was sold. That captain has never tired of acknowledging the hospitality shown by the natives on the occasion.

The contrast is remarkable, and nothing need be said to emphasize it. The difference is as between brutalized heathens and Christianized men.

## CHAPTER XVII.
### How Tongoan Christians Die.

Manamoana's Vision—Manaura's Testimony—Tinabua's Peace.

ONE of the first of the natives to show an interest in the Gospel was a Panita man named Manamoana. He was a quiet pleasant-looking individual, and one day after a Gospel service, said to the missionary, "O misi! these are good words you are telling us. There is life in them. Most of our people let them go into one ear, but they also let them go out of the other. These are not words we should allow to go out again."

Mr. Michelsen rejoiced to see that the Word of God was reaching the poor man's heart, and was disposed to anticipate help in the work from one who had thus early become an attentive listener. He was sorry, however, not many weeks afterwards, to hear that the man was seriously ill. Going to his house, he ascertained the facts. Rather than talk about his health, however, the man, pointing heavenwards, desired Mr. Michelsen " to speak to the Great One up there." After prayer, he remarked: " Oh, that is good! Speak to Him again for me." This was done, and at his request again repeated.

## "The Angels have come for me!"

Frequent and prolonged visits were paid by the missionary to the dying man, and the way of salvation explained to his delighted soul. On the last occasion, though very weak and exhausted, he suddenly sprang up on the bed, and excitedly pointing to the door, said: "Don't you see them?"

Mr. Michelsen asked: "What do you see?"

Again pointing, he said: "Do you not see the angels there? They have come for me."

Mr. Michelsen, desirous of calming the man, said: "Wait a little; your time has not yet come."

Induced to lie down, Manamoana continued peering through the door.

After a hasty dinner, Mr. Michelsen proceeded again to the poor man's house; but was no sooner outside than he heard the familiar death-wail. The rapturous vision of angel-hosts was speedily followed by Manamoana's spirit being recalled by "the Great One up there." At the house the hired women-mourners were sitting round the corpse, continuing their lamentations.

Manaura,[*] senior chief of Mangarisu, one of the party who escorted Mr. Michelsen through the bush on the occasion of the flight to Selembanga, had been a notoriously wicked man. He had probably caused more people to be killed and eaten than any other man on the island in his generation. He was said to have had as many as fifty wives. Should any one offend him and flee from his village, a message followed the fugitive, instructing the chief under whose

---

[*] He was a thin, hunchbacked man, with sharp features. He occupies second place in the procession of engraving on page 67.

protection he might be to "kill him and eat him"! Rather than insult Manaura, fellow-chiefs would unhesitatingly obey such a command.

On one occasion, in early life, a brother of this chief aroused his wrath. Manaura sent to Selembanga—where the culprit was living—orders that he should be buried alive. Manambalea, his half-brother, who was then but a boy of seven or eight years, was made to hold the torch for the grave-digger in the man's house—a dark hut. The man was compelled to go into the grave, and two of his wives went with him. All three were buried alive! Such was Manaura's influence as a "sacred" chief, that no one dared to interfere. This man's life was made up of deeds of cruelty and blood. At last he became very ill. At the request of Mr. Michelsen, Manambalea invited his kinsman over to Selembanga, in order that he might receive medical attention at the mission house. The invitation was accepted, and Manambalea conveyed him on his back.

Whilst, however, efforts to benefit the body failed, other influences were more successfully brought to bear upon him. By the blessing of God, Manaura was led to repentance for his sins of ignorance and wickedness, and to find in Jesus the Great Saviour whom he needed.

When the old man's son and other heathen friends saw that death was near, they entered the mission house by night and removed him. Their object was to bury him with heathen rites and ceremonies. While Manaura continued to live, both Manambalea and Mr. Michelsen frequently visited him in his own village, and were much cheered by what they saw and heard.

His son, however, did not cease to maintain the advantage of being buried as "a great chief," rather than to be put in the ground at the mission station with nothing attending the proceedings beyond a religious service. What was this in comparison with a feast—an eating of pigs and a drinking of *kava*\*—extending over at least a hundred days!

Dressed in a garment with which the missionary had presented him, the lingering invalid would come out of his hut, and listen to the Word of God as it was preached in the village. He also used his influence to get others to listen. Sad to say, however, he never had the opportunities for good which allowed of such vigorous action as he formerly showed in the service of sin and Satan. This was his grief.

At last he died. During the closing moments, heathen acquaintances surrounded him, and talked of the grand feast they would make in his honour after death. Six months previously this would have carried his sympathies, and have satisfied all his ambition. Now, however, his only remark was—"Jesus!" They told him how much they wished him to die as he had lived in former years—a heathen; and to be buried with the same pomp and display as his ancestors. Moreover, in the course of a year or two, a memorial feast—such as never had been held before on Tongoa for magnificence—would be held, with dancing and other accompaniments. These things had no longer any charm for Manaura, who answered every argument with the word—"Jesus!" No other name had in it the music which could "refresh the soul in death" of that

---

\* See description, page 136.

weary, worn-out—but penitent—sinner! His friends afterwards told the missionary: "He said just one word—that word you always talk about—'Jesus!'"

Tinabua, nephew of Malakaleo, was a firm friend of the Mission; and it was mainly through his influence that the mission house was put up at Lumbukuti. Quiet and thoughtful, slow to act and speak, and of a peaceful disposition, he did not say much about Gospel-work; but his heart seemed increasingly drawn to the Word of God.

Early in 1890 he was taken ill; and although it was difficult to say that anything serious was the matter with him, he grew weaker and weaker. On a bad cough being followed by a condition which was hopeless, he was told that his end was drawing near. He sank very rapidly. Asked whether he was prepared to face Jesus—the Saviour and Judge—he articulated the simple word—*Tamate* \* (Peace).

"Are you quite sure that you have laid all your sins on Jesus, and that you are saved by Him?"

In the midst of great suffering he answered the same word—"Peace."

Not many hours afterwards he slept in peace. Few among the natives were better instructed than that young chief, who never missed an opportunity to learn of God and the plan of salvation.

---

\* An interesting word, signifying that calmness which often characterizes the *Pacific* Ocean.

## CHAPTER XVIII.
## Some Tongoan "Institutions."

Infanticide — Circumcision — Polygamy — *Kava*-Drinking — Commemoration of the Dead—Sacred stones—Chieftainship—Installation of Timataso—The New Chief Commended to God—The Queensland Labour Traffic—United Action—" Rocks Ahead !"

INFANTICIDE was very common on the island when Mr. Michelsen went. It cannot have been practised for many generations, however, or the people would not have been so numerous. It is very likely that it dates from the time when the Queensland traffic was commenced. This parted husbands and wives for several years, and infanticide (more often pre-natal) was an expedient to put away the evidences of unfaithfulness on the part of the women. Once introduced, the practice became general.

In spite of constant wars, the population of the island must have increased steadily from the time of original settlement, in the sixteenth century, up to about fifty years ago, when it was probably three times as large as at present. During the past generation there has been a continual decrease. For this, infanticide and the Kanaka traffic are mainly responsible. The natural resources are equal to a population ten times as large as the present, which is a little over a thousand. Since the introduction of Christianity, infanticide has ceased; and in some of the villages a large number of women fondle babies on their arms.

Among the social practices—of no definite religious significance on Tongoa — is circumcision. Though very general on some of the islands, it is only observed by a section of the population of our island; and then not in infancy, but when about twelve or fourteen years of age. It is not a caste badge, but very probably a survival of a tribal custom. There are, on some of the islands, more indications of caste than appear on Tongoa.

The polygamous practices of the people have been a great drawback to Gospel work. Chiefs and others of an ambitious turn of mind, have spared no effort to increase the number of their wives; others have added them to their households as "women" to do their bidding.

Although making it a rule not to baptize polygamists, Mr. Michelsen has ever distinguished between preaching the Gospel and merely denouncing sinful customs. Though speaking against polygamy, and not withholding clear statements regarding the moral law, he has put his strength into making known the Gospel, before which alone the evil ways of the people must fall into ill-favour. In his own words: "I did not persuade them to put away their wives—I left the truth to do its own purifying work. I make it clear to them that polygamy is not God's holy way, but a practice which sin has brought into the world."

"Putting Away" his Wives.

And the truth *has* done its purifying work. Once at Epi Mr. Michelsen addressed a large and hearty meeting of several villages. On that occasion he said nothing about polygamy; but, after the gathering, he saw a cluster of people, one of whom was speaking very loud, almost excitedly. On inquiry, the missionary was told that a man wished to put away his wives! The simple fact was, that the Gospel had reached the man's heart; but the poor fellow could not look up to God, because of the sinful manner of life that interposed between himself and the Holy One.

In some countries the social customs are such that the natives have to face many perplexing questions on proposing to put away their wives. Not so in the island of Tongoa, where, under the old order, a woman was as well off without a husband as with one. Women have their own plantations, so they need not starve. In many cases they are thankful to be free—marriage is bond-service; and to be "put away" often amounts to having their liberty given them!

The wives of a Tongoan chief were expected to serve him as he might direct. Chiefs were held in honour according to their capacity to buy "women." A chief would have a number of houses—one for himself, and one for each of his wives. In the event of a man dying, the wife or wives passed over to his brother, somewhat after an arrangement which God suffered to obtain among the ancient Israelites.

Marriages were arranged by parents even while the parties were infants. Thus, a boy who was to be a chief had many wives bespoken for him. The girl was paid for—so many pigs. As there was much ambition among parents for their girls to be the wives of chiefs, the proposal generally emanated from the feminine side. Since the influence of Christianity has been felt on the island, these hateful customs have fallen into disrepute. Marriages are now arranged by the young men and maidens themselves; and some interest attaches to the fact that the right to open the question is not the exclusive privilege of the stronger sex.

*Kava* is a stupefying drink, common in the islands. There are various methods of preparing it; all of them essentially objectionable, and in their outcome decidedly hurtful. It is prepared from the root of *piper methysticum*, and the process is attended by a peculiar ceremony. Standing up in a circle, the men of Tongoa took a leaf, and laid it upon the opening formed by the thumb and first finger of the left hand, and then struck it with the palm of the right. This was an act of "sacrificing to the spirits." Exclaiming "*Natamate*" ("spirits of the dead"), the Kava devotees practically dedicated the drink to the entire spirit-world. To the "spirits" they gave the useless leaves; their own sensual tastes were indulged by the use of the root.

The root was cut into small pieces, which were distributed among men, who masticated them in their mouths. The pulp was spit out, squeezed in a cup, and repeatedly chewed by one after another of the company; then it was strained through fibre of the cocoa-nut husk. Retiring to the corners of the square surrounding the Kava-house—and every village had such an institution—so as not to be seen in the act, the men drank the filthy liquid.

This drink induces a variety of stomach troubles, and causes the death of many people. While unable to urge upon uninstructed heathens the sinfulness of the practice because of its association with spirit-worship, the missionary boldly declared the habit sinful, because it interferes with the natural functions, and destroys the human body.

There is no trace of a holy day having been observed on Tongoa before the Gospel introduced the Sabbath of the Lord. Feasts over the dead—such as are known as "wakes" in some parts of the British Empire—were frequent. The bodies of the dead were dressed up and painted, and kept until decomposition had so far advanced as to necessitate burial. The body symbolized the spiritual presence of the departed one at the feast in his honour. Every tenth day during the mourning, and in commemorations in after years, was invested with a special character. There may in this be the survival of a periodical festival.

Sacred stones, which were inserted in belts, were held to protect their wearers from many evils. These charms were handed down from one generation to another as heirlooms and tokens for good. Some of the sacred men had large numbers of them, which they "worked" in connection with various "arts." Needless to say, they expected reward for their divination. Moreover, at the season of planting it was customary to put into the ground stones, similar in shape to the expected fruit, which were supposed to act as charms, and influence the harvest.

Chieftainship is hereditary, designation also. If a chief

dies, and his son is an infant, the chief's brother, with the consent of the people, assumes authority until such time as the young man may " come of age." It is the rule for chiefs, when advancing in years, to introduce their sons to the responsibilities of office. In such cases the senior chief guides the junior in his work.

The great work of the chief in heathen days was the ordering of feasts. Ruling was nothing to this—indeed, this amounted to good ruling. When a man gets old, he is glad to make these duties devolve upon younger shoulders, to whom, as a rule, they are less irksome and more agreeable.

The young man Timataso\* was installed as Tinabua, on the death of Malakalco's immediate successor. The ceremony was of an essentially Christian character. A shed was erected adjoining the church at Lumbukuti, to hold the great crowd that assembled to witness the proceedings. In compliance with the desire of the chief-elect, the people were in mourning for the late chief— an arrangement never known before, but showing a fine trait in the disposition of Timataso. In some measure the ceremony was a working out of the old custom; but the whole was characterized by a becoming solemnity.

Not only were all the villagers present, but all the chiefs of the island, and a large number of other people as well. The relation of the chief to the people, and the responsibility of the chief as such to God, were explained in detail by the missionary. As an innovation, it was made clear that the chief does not *own* the people, but is their head; and should be a ruler

---

\* See note on p. 68.

of willing subjects. It was also shown that it is as a servant of God that the chief is called upon to act.

The presence of other chiefs was in honour of an old custom, which, however, had in the past only been partially carried out. Because of the constant wars between the various villages, no such complete re-union had before been possible. It is the rule on Tongoa for the young chief to receive office from the retiring chief: as the last chief of Lumbukuti had died, his predecessor was again called in to act as "retiring chief."

The installation ceremony began with all the villagers coming up to the new chief and pressing his hand—the imported form of greeting—and promising to be faithful subjects of Tinabua, who, on his part, engaged to rule them for their happiness. This was a new element in the ceremony, as formerly the chief was regarded as the rightful *owner* of the people! This part of the programme—somewhat tedious, it is true—was followed by Malakaleo transferring the chieftainship by laying his hand upon the young man, and saying, "Be thou Tinabua." After that, Tinabua joined hands with all the other chiefs, forming a circle round the missionary and Malakaleo—implying that he was not only the chief of Lumbukuti, but one of the federation of chiefs on Tongoa, and accepted by them as a brother ruler.

"There is no power but of God; and the powers that be are ordained of God." In recognition of this important truth, the missionary engaged in prayer, asking the King of kings and Lord of lords graciously to accept the services of Tinabua, and to bless his efforts to make the people of Lumbukuti happy through the fear of God. The singing of a hymn concluded the ceremony. A feast worthy of the chief's influence, and in harmony with the auspicious event, followed. The installation thus described in detail is one of several that have taken place on the island since Christianity has asserted its power there.

The idea of oneness of interest and obligation on the part of the chiefs, suggested by their joining hands during these installation proceedings, is more and more taking a practical turn. On one occasion, the chiefs conferred together regarding the Queensland Labour Traffic, and decided to petition the Governor of the Colony, protesting against the Kanaka "recruiting," which is such a scourge to the Islands. They thought he might respect their rights over their people; and they duly appointed a scribe, who prepared a memorial which they all signed. This was then translated by the missionary, and forwarded to the authorities in Queensland. To the unspeakable delight of all, the petition was respected; and no "recruiting" has since been done on Tongoa.

Another instance of united effort is furnished by a more recent occurrence, during the absence of the missionary from the island, while on furlough. One day, while H.M.S. *Dart*—Captain Frederick in charge—was at anchor at Tongoa, all the chiefs went on board. Tinabua was the spokesman, and in quite creditable English he explained to the Captain that the inhabitants feared "rocks ahead" in regard to European influence. Having seen the benefits of British protection in the Fiji Islands—and doubtless also having their feelings stirred up through the Christian and gentlemanly conduct of Captain Frederick and his officers—they begged that Her Majesty might be petitioned to take the people under her benign protection.* The Captain undertook to convey their views to the Foreign Office. The chiefs of Emae, hearing what had been done, speedily made for Tongoa, and presented a similar request.

As another illustration of the native confidence in British rule and care, mention may be made of a childish expression on the part of the eldest son of Marimaraki, the chief of Pélé. The missionary had just received a beautiful picture of the Queen and the Royal Family; and this was shown to the young man and some other natives as—"our Chief and her Family." After admiring the numerous and interesting group, the youth exclaimed: "If they are so many as all that, why does she not send one of them to Tongoa?" That is, as Governor, of course! Conscious of their individual weakness, the chiefs of the island gladly combine for strength; but, even then, they feel the need of resting, if possible, upon the powerful arm of Imperial Britain.

---

* Would that the inhabitants of the New Hebrides were as happily situated as the Fijians! At a Missionary Conference held at Aneityum, in June, 1892, it was resolved:—"The Synod, having heard with alarm of the threatened early annexation of these islands by France, and feeling that such annexation would be ruinous to our work, and to the best interests of the natives generally, urges upon the Presbyterian churches of Britain to use their influence with Her Majesty's Government to prevent such annexation." At the meeting in 1891, a similar resolution was recorded.

## CHAPTER XIX.
## A Question of Custom.

Serious Dispute on Epi—Great Victory for Christian Honour—
Noble Determination of the Natives.

JUST about the time of the return of the refugees to Epi, Manambalca again showed himself an advocate of peace principles on the basis of the Gospel. He heard that some of the other villages of Epi speaking the Tasiko language were at war. Taking with him, as interpreter, a Tasiko man, who happened to be on Tongoa, he went to the troubled region, and made peace between the contending parties. *Shortly afterwards these people applied for teachers!* At the time, the villages were under the charge of Rev. R. M. Fraser; so Mr. Michelsen could do nothing. One of the villages in Epi, by name Tonomia, the strongest in that part, kept back until 1891, and then it seemed less likely than formerly to admit Christian influence. In the meantime the villages had come into Mr. Michelsen's care. An event then occurred, which proved the beginning of a new era. A woman had left the village to become the wife of a man belonging to another village—to which a teacher had been sent. She was asked to go back, but refused; and the man likewise was not willing to part with her. At the same time, he did not seem disposed to discharge the alternative obligation—so many pigs!

Mr. Michelsen had gone over to Epi, just at that time, determined, if possible, to see the last heathen village in his district placed under Christian instruction —so to give practical effect to the labours and prayers of many years. Hearing of the trouble respecting the woman, he made for the village which was determined to compel its neighbour to observe a well-known custom regarding payment for wives received from other tribes. After a long walk through the bush, the village was reached. Only a youth was to be seen, and he explained that the men had gone into the forest. He led the way; and a mile or so distant, Mr. Michelsen came upon the tribe in fighting order under the shade of some enormous trees. All had guns, except the few old men who were not so far advanced in "civilization": they were armed, some with bows and poisoned arrows, others with spears.

The missionary was received in a friendly manner. Explaining to him the reason of the hostilities that were in progress, the leaders said that the "Christian" people had been dealing unjustly with them. The injustice complained of lay in the fact that pressure had not been brought to bear upon the man who took a wife from Tonomia without paying for her. Mr. Michelsen proposed a visit to the offending village, in order to a friendly conference. Armed men were not likely to look kindly upon such a suggestion; and, in fact, it was at once ruled out of the question. To be sure, it would involve a moral courage which is not necessarily cultivated by the engagements of the field of battle. Brave to fight, the forces of Tonomia hesitated to face the foe on any other terms.

A little reason having been brought to bear, Mr. Michelsen succeeded in persuading the men to go with him. At the other village they found a divided feeling. The chief, who was a decided Christian, would like to have the matter settled peaceably. The man who had taken the woman, as well as some of his friends, did not put in an appearance. At last they were found, and made to face the facts.

These facts were set forth by the missionary in an address to this effect: Whatever you do, you should live at peace with one another. No lasting peace can exist where there is unfair dealing. The woman went away from her village, and became the wife of a man whom she wished to have, and who wished to have her. So far, all right. According to heathen custom, if a woman leaves one village to go to another, the former village expects to receive some compensation from the village which gains a new resident. When you all become Christians—here and there also—payment will not be made for any woman. But Tonomia, which is yet heathen, expects payment for the woman. So I say that you must pay the usual price, or the woman must go back again! The last clause was strongly emphasized; and the key-note, thus sounded, guided the proceedings, and carried the day. The chief was quite willing for the woman to go back; but the husband wished to retain her. At the same time he seemed unable to pay the price—ten or fifteen pigs!

## "The Gun ate him!"

Several speeches followed, all in favour of peace. A heathen stood up, and, pointing to a boy, said: "Where is that boy's father? The gun ate him!" He proceeded: "Look at that young man. Where is his brother? The gun ate him!" And so on, naming a large number whose relatives had been killed in war. All agreed that the villages ought to live in peace. Moreover, it was affirmed all round that this could not be until all became Christian!

After two hours the warriors of Tonomia left, with the understanding that the woman would be paid for. Next morning the missionary heard that there had been some difficulty in getting together a sufficient number of pigs. Thereupon he sent a message in these terms: "Then the woman must go back." This had the desired effect, and the obligation was discharged the next day. The pigs on such occasions are generally served up at a village feast.

A teacher was then settled in Tonomia—the only village in the district that remained entirely heathen. Mr. Michelsen has several times heard of the progress of his work there. It is joyous to relate that everything goes to confirm the remarkable promise that was made when the teacher was settled: "We are determined to make up for lost time." Education and evangelization are being zealously promoted, with the earnest co-operation of the people.

That was the last battle with open heathenism, fought by Mr. Michelsen in the district allotted to him by the Mission Synod.

K

## CHAPTER XX.
## Present Condition of the Mission.

Extent of the Work and its Needs—Singing—Communication between the Islands and Australasia—Statement by Mr. Michelsen.

THE work around which these incidents cluster has expanded to such an extent that there were, in January, 1893, four stations in Mr. Michelsen's district—two on Tongoa, one on Tongariki, and one on Epi. The missionary stays at the stations alternately, spending most of his time at the head station at Lumbukuti.

The villages of the entire district number 32, with a population of 2070. There are no heathen; the people have been Christianized. The church membership in June, 1891, when Mr. Michelsen left for a period of furlough, was 194. False professors are becoming more and more unhappy, and true believers increasingly earnest.

Weekly collections, in the direction of self-support, have recently been commenced. As much as 16s., in pennies and half-pennies, has been taken at a single meeting at Lumbukuti from 200 people. If the same

## The Lumbukuti Station. 147

result were attained throughout the district, the mission would be self-supporting. The realization of this may be in the distant future; but there is reason to believe that the hope is not utopian.

Not all at once did the educational work assume its present advanced shape and importance. Some of the first teachers that were sent out were young, and more zealous than wise. When people would not attend

NEW HEAD STATION AT LUMBUKUTI.

school, these advocates of "compulsory education" discussed means to force them! To-day the majority of the people can read, and many can write. The enlarged district, including part of Epi, has a population of over two thousand.

While in many parts of the Group teachers are urgently needed, so far as Mr. Michelsen's own district is concerned this is not the case, for every village has its teacher. Of course, these humble workers have not had a seminary training; but there is a prospect of the standard of efficiency being raised in the future, for Rev. Robt. Lamb, M.D., is about to open an institution for the higher education of islanders at Ambrim. It is hoped that, after a course of suitable training, the teachers of the future will be equipped for assuming larger responsibilities. This, in the first place, would do much towards reducing the force of European missionaries; and, in the second place, it might be the stepping-stone to the formation of a native ministry.

Not without much effort has the present condition of things been attained. Mr. Michelsen had, generally speaking, to educate his teachers before he could have their services. If it had been possible, in the early days of the mission, to procure from neighbouring missions an adequate number of teachers, the present happy state of things on Tongoa would, humanly speaking, have been anticipated by a period of several years.

The Roman Catholic priests have already arrived in the Group, and are doing their utmost to establish their footing. The traffic in strong drink by unscrupulous traders is also a crying evil. An urgent need is a Missionary reinforcement that shall work all the islands, and by advancing the Gospel and true civilization, enable the people to withstand Romish superstition and other snares and temptations.

Singing has exercised a useful ministry on the island. The first attendants at the school eagerly picked up the hymns that were sung to them. To the great joy of the missionary, the Gospel story went before him in

## Christian Chiefs.          149

the songs which thus travelled from village to village. Wherever he went he heard hymns; walking to their plantations or at their work, the people were singing Christian melodies instead of the old heathen songs, which were, almost without exception, impure.

Through the operations of the Australian United Steam Navigation Company, there is constant com-

1 Eldest son of Marimaraki.  2 The late Tinabua.  3 Tarisaliu.  4 Matabuti.
5 Maritariliu.  6 Samori.  7 Manambalea.
A GROUP OF CHRISTIAN CHIEFS.

munication between the Islands and Australasia. A small steamer performs the inter-island service; and once a month a large steamer leaves Sydney for the Islands, advancing healthy trade among the populations. The Australian New Hebrides Company, another medium of communication, is being worked by Christian men in Australia, who are concerned about the development of wholesome commerce with the natives, with a view to helping the Missions.*

The contrast between the past and present has thus been stated by Mr. Michelsen himself:—

"Cannibalism is now a thing of the past; the Prince of Peace reigns over two thousand natives, who from time immemorial had lived in almost uninterrupted war. Souls enslaved with chains of superstition are set free indeed, for the Son has made them free. Selfishness and hatred are fast vanishing before the rising Sun of Righteousness, which now on many an occasion brings former enemies together in the name of Jesus, to 'show forth the Lord's death till He come.'

"Once a week, believers from every part of the island meet to study the Word of God under the missionary's guidance. From almost every house in the whole district, at the dawn of day, silence is broken by the song of praise. From one dwelling is heard the well-known words of 'All people that on earth do dwell,' in the native language; from another, 'There is a Name I love to hear'; perhaps from another, the 23rd Psalm or the 121st; or 'Rock of Ages, cleft for me.'

"Then they have prayer. As this usually takes place before there is sufficient light to see to read, there is no reading of the Word until the meetings for morning school and worship. Where the evenings were spent in idle, and worse than idle, talk, the people are now gathered in groups round the light of a modern lamp

---

* These established means of communication explain the importance of all letters for the Islands being addressed "*viâ* Sydney."

## Spiritual Activity.

in every house, reading, singing, and uniting in prayer. The aged are cared for,* and infant lives are spared. In every village, where formerly men and women had feasts—each sex in turn dancing round their heathen drums,† singing songs that were the product of an impure heart, and spending the whole night in the vilest revelry—to-day is to be seen the entire population going up to the house of the Lord, and each village strives to excel the other in spiritual activity; whilst former enemies are never forgotten in their prayers.

"Most of the people have learned to read; and very satisfactory progress is being made in the knowledge of the Word of God. Not only have the natives throughout the district shown themselves ready to speak a word for Jesus; but in many instances have wrought with their hands in the erection of schools and churches, with no less zeal than that which they formerly exhibited in preparation for their heathen and carnal feasts. Some have gone forth to other islands, taking their lives in their hands for the sake of making known to the heathen the unsearchable riches of Christ; and many more are waiting to be fully instructed for the work.

---

* In former times, the aged, when unable to provide for themselves, were frequently left to die of hunger in desolate huts. To bury them alive was suggested by feelings of comparative pity—as less harsh than cold neglect.

† These were in clusters, or "groves," recalling the Canaanitish abominations "in every high hill, and under every green tree." They were often erected under large banyan trees. Interchange of clothing by the sexes, and other details of obscenity such as characterized the worship of Baal-Ashtoreth, were not unknown on the island. See engraving on page 36.

## Present Condition of the Mission.

"In former days their greatest desire in death was that they might be buried with due heathen honours. In recent times many have died fearing no evil—for 'Thou art with me.' But whilst praising God for what He *has* done, I earnestly invite the reader to join in the prayer that past experiences may be as nothing in the light of future blessings, but that unparalleled numbers of such as are already nominal and outward Christians may be called forth into the eternal life in Jesus, and be led to exclaim: 'Behold, what manner of love the Father hath bestowed upon us, that we should be called the children of God; *and such we are.*'"

---

**Extract from letter by "Billy," a Christian Teacher on Tongariki.**

(Peculiarities in pronunciation: Vowels as in German; $g$ = ng; $d$ = nd; $\bar{p}$ = gbw; $p$ also does duty for $b$.)

*Misi, Taro paki Togariki. Tea ni Lakilia teu po do marama nanoai eu doronawoo ana go Nagoroi eu da moro simoko Maleisere I mate; go tea lapa eu punusia go eu mataku; go teu po saisai pia. Au dodamimu nalakena ku moro soki gami ganosiano ki Lupe; go au laelae. Io, te nou. Kinau Pili*

### TRANSLATION.

Misi, We two have gone to Tongariki. The people of Lakilia are being affected by the Light; the men no longer become stinking [*i.e.*, intoxicated], and the women no longer smoke. Maleisere is dead; the many saw it, and feared; and they are now coming out well to the meetings. . . . Our hearts are drawn out to you, because you again press upon us the urgency of the work of God, and we rejoice. Yes, that is all.

I (am), Billy.

## CHAPTER XXI.
### The Queensland Kanaka Traffic.

The word "Kanaka"—The "Third Plague"—Tongoa free from the Scourge—Deplorable Facts—"Finis" inevitable.

SEVERAL allusions have already been made to the Kanaka Traffic, on which a brief statement must now suffice. The word *Kanaka* means "a man" in the Hawaiian and other islands; in the Samoa and Maori languages it is *Tanga-ta*; and in Tongoan, *Na-ata*, or, in designating the people of a village, *Na-ka*. So the Kanaka traffic means a traffic in *human beings*!

After the whaling and sandal-wood trades, the Kanaka traffic has come in as the third plague in the New Hebrides. It began about 1863. There is no need to rehearse in these pages the horrors of the traffic; others have made it their business to bring these before the free citizens of the British Empire. Nor is it asserted that the Kanaka traffic is the same to-day as when the *Carl* and similar atrocities were perpetrated some twenty-five years ago. Women as well as men are by it deported to labour in the sugar plantations of Queensland.

On representations from the missionaries and other friends of the natives, the traffic has been regulated more and more stringently during the past twenty years; and it may almost be said that nothing more can be done for the protection of the natives, *so long as the traffic continues to be sanctioned.* A Queensland Government Agent is found on board every "recruiting" vessel; ships of war are cruising about the Islands ready to enforce due observance of the regulations—and splendid work has been done by this means by Captain Davies and other faithful servants of the Queen. The opinion prevails among friends of the natives that the traffic *cannot be further regulated.*

I do not assert that all the regulations are carried out; indeed, if the "recruits" were not paid for, in cash or kind, to the chiefs of the villages, or others who may be considered as owning them, the natives would regard the traffic as man-stealing, and bloodshed would inevitably attend its pursuit. Owing to the united action of the chiefs of the island, as described on p. 140, Tongoa has of late enjoyed complete immunity from the scourge.

The deplorable fact is that the traffic takes the greater part of the young, strong men of the Islands away from their homes, leaving their wives unprotected. They are engaged for periods of from three years to nine or ten, but in the majority of cases do not return; instead of welcoming their husbands back, poor women only receive the news of their death in a strange land. These circumstances are productive of immorality, and probably gave rise—as is mentioned elsewhere—to the fearful destruction of infant life, now so common on all

## A Sad Fact.

the heathen islands. In a great many of the villages few people are seen besides women and old men, and a very small number of children. The able-bodied men, who ought to be the strength of the Islands and the strength of the mission, are in Queensland. Only about a third of them return home; the other two-thirds die in the colony. Moreover, the fact should not be overlooked that natives suffering from consumption or other incurable diseases, are frequently sent home simply to die.

It is often said that the native races "die when they come into contact with civilization." This does not adequately explain the high rate of Kanaka mortality in Queensland. White men often pronounce the natives "lazy"; if inclined to dispute the correctness of the statement, I should say that my observation is, that in their plantations at home the natives work as much as they are physically able—that is, probably eight hours a day. In Queensland they are made to labour as no European could under the same climatic conditions; and that is much beyond their capacity. It is very doubtful if the South Sea Islanders can, without injury to health, do more work in the colony than a European.

Queensland planters object to coolies and Chinese, who are able to work in the climate without serious injury to themselves; doubtless the objection arises from the fact that this class of labour would not pay so well. If the Kanakas were only expected to work according to *their* strength, it is probable that they would be the less profitable class of labourers. It seems clear that the margin of profit for the planters lies between what the Kanakas are able to bear, and what they are not able to bear, but yet are made to do.

In other words, the profit of the sugar planter is proportionate to the number of Kanakas worked to death.

An incident will help us to realize what this traffic is doing for the Islands. I was once sailing with some Tanna men from Port Resolution (Dr. J. G. Paton's first station) to Futuna. Conversing with the men in broken English, I inquired if there were many people then living about Port Resolution. One of the party laconically answered, "*Pinis*" ("Finish"). That was to say, there were none! Many a Government agent, when asked if the traffic would soon be stopped, has remarked: "Really, it does not much matter; for if it is not stopped, it will soon stop itself." This, I believe, is true. If the traffic is not discontinued, a period of twenty or thirty years may suffice to end it; and to witness the return of a Kanaka ship to the colonies with the sad report—"*Pinis*"!

## CHAPTER XXII.
## Notes and Incidents.

Tongoans as Warriors — Waiting for the Gospel — A Curious Caution — Pulling down the Hurricane — Dawn of Christian Reform — The Currency of Tongoa — Merciful Deliverances — Native Cunning and Simplicity—"The Pharisee and the Publican" — The "Wine" of Tongoa — The Languages of Mr. Michelsen's District—Tongoans and "The Blessed Hope"— Saved to Save—"That's what 'the Light' does for us!"

THE courage and enterprise which led to the first settlement of Tongoa, some 300 years ago, after the great volcanic disaster, seems to have been maintained to the present time; although old men complain that those of the younger generation are not equal to their fathers. There is not a village on the island without a long story of bloody battles fought.

It often happened that when walking through the forests, places were pointed out to Mr. Michelsen as former sites of various villages. The Pele people have been driven from their place once since Mr. Michelsen went to the island; the Lumbukuti tribe were just building their new villages when he arrived, after living several years at Panita. Even the Selembanga men were driven off their land; and so with Mangarisu and Kurumambe. Tarisaliu, that cruel cannibal of Purau, was driven from his place three times during Mr. Michelsen's residence.

This, of course, is only the negative side of the matter. But it implies the other. Nor has their warfare always been confined to their own island. Thus, several years ago, a wife of Ti-Tongoa (afterwards called Manaura), on leaving Queensland, where she had been engaged in sugar plantation work, did not return to her own island. During her stay in Queensland, she had consorted with a man from Siviri, on Efate. It is a very common thing for women, during their three years' stay in the colony, to be wives of other men. Knowing what a cruel master her rightful owner was, the woman preferred to go ashore with her *pro tem.* Efatese husband. This fact was soon reported to Ti-Tongoa, who called together all his friends on Tongoa, and even some from other islands, and, after a feast, laid the matter before them. They agreed to go and bring the woman back.

Fifty canoes were fitted up. They set out on their voyage of over thirty miles one afternoon, came up to Efate in the night, and had the village surrounded by fighting-men when the people emerged from their huts in the morning. Though savages, they did not lose sight of their real object, *i.e.*, to get the woman back. Before attacking the people, they made known the purpose of their visit. The Siviri people thought prudence the better part of valour, and gladly delivered up the woman, with a reasonable number of pigs as war indemnity. The invading Islanders returned

## Waiting for the Gospel.

the next day, satisfied with the result. They had also left a lasting impression on the minds of the people of Efate, who never again ventured to offend the Tongoans.

Years before Mr. Michelsen went to Tongoa, news reached the island of the settlement of missionaries on Efate. This did not affect the general population; but there was one upon whose mind it made a deep impression—a woman named Leinasu. She made all possible inquiries, and earnestly longed to hear the good news from the mouths of the missionaries.

This woman had a kind of presentiment that she should live to see the day when "the Light" would be known in the island. She passed through much suffering and many trials. Her husband was shot in one of the wars, and she herself carried home his body to save it from being eaten by the enemy. Fleeing from the savage bush village to which she belonged, she took refuge in Selembanga.

No sooner did Leinasu learn that a missionary had arrived, than she sought the knowledge for which she had so long been thirsting. She was one of the first on that side of the island to embrace the Gospel, and was for some years the faithful servant of Mr. and Mrs. Michelsen. Her quiet Christian conduct and kindly bearing were influential in a high degree.

Telling her own story, she has often said that before finding peace through believing in Christ, she trembled at the thought of her sins. This statement is the more remarkable because a sense of sin is not readily admitted by the natives. But this woman's conviction was such as to impress her with the exceeding sinfulness of sin. She afterwards became the wife of an earnest Christian teacher on the island.

During the first year Mr. Michelsen was on Tongoa he proposed a visit to the village of Sakau, on the island of Epi. Some native boys asked to accompany him, and were allowed to do so. One questioned the missionary as to what he was going to do. The answer was: *Lotu*—" Worship." "Well," said the youth, "let us pray when we get there, but *do not let us shut our eyes*; for the Epians are not to be trusted!" This is not altogether a new version of " *Watch* and pray."

Mr. Michelsen rejoiced to find, however, that the story of Jesus, the Way to Eternal Life, made a profound impression upon the minds of the people. When they heard of the glory in store for those who trust in Jesus, several interrupted and exclaimed, "Let's all go there!"

There is a grim interest in the story of Ti-Tongoa and the hurricane which he claimed to command. While yet a heathen, this "sacred" chief invited the chief of Euta to a feast. The invitation was not accepted, on the ground that the proceedings would be simply heathen. Thereupon Ti-Tongoa conceived coercive measures.

"If you will not come," he said, "I will pull down the hurricane upon you."

A terrible threat, unquestionably; but still the chief of Euta declined. Not many days afterwards the hurricane came, and did fearful damage. Curiously enough, however, its strength was spent upon Ti-Tongoa's land. The grounds of neighbouring chiefs, being sheltered, suffered very little.

Meeting Ti-Tongoa about that time, the missionary charged him with having brought on a hurricane. The impeachment was stoutly denied. Carrying his banter a step further, Mr. Michelsen added: "You said yourself you would pull down a hurricane; and it would seem that you pulled the wrong string." To this Ti-Tongoa made no reply. He is now of a different temper. Being thoughtful, he exercises a good influence on the island.

The Sabbatarian zeal of the good chief, Manambalea, led him once to a curious expedient. Tongoans have an appetite for fowls; and Manambalea, preparing for a Sunday dinner, had to face the question of dressing and cooking the fowl. He saw no objection to the dinner being provided on Sunday, and then the fowl could be killed. In the meantime, however, it could be plucked! At this operation, Mr. Michelsen was horrified to find one of the chief's servants engaged on the previous Saturday!

The fowl was screeching wildly; and on the missionary looking out, the lad ceased his work, and the fowl stalked about in a nakedness which was painful to witness. The lad explained that Manambalea did not want to make too much work on Sunday! The incident showed a savage thoughtlessness rather than a savage intention. The missionary thus had to inculcate lessons of mercy, as well as rules for pious living.

In the early days of the Mission, all dealings with the natives were conducted by means of barter; and as Mr. Michelsen has had sometimes as many as fifty natives to support—catechumens and intending teachers—there was much "dealing" to do. In fact, nearly half the missionary's time was spent in procuring things needful for the large household.

To simplify such transactions, he made some signed tickets, which were received by the people as money; and afterwards "honoured" on presentation — some being of the nominal value of a halfpenny, and others of one penny. Shrewd half-heathens soon hit upon the idea of "making money" by splitting these cards—overlooking the fact that the missionary's initials were on one side only. Moreover, this perishable "coin" was found unserviceable. The next step was to introduce English money; and this civilized form of exchange speedily became an established institution on Tongoa. Much disappointment is prevented, and time is economized in a very satisfactory manner.

"Some trust in princes," but Mr. Michelsen has not had any such uncertain protection. British and French vessels cruise about the islands, to guard European interests; but it is a remarkable fact, that only once, from the day when he first landed on Tongoa, until all the villages had been placed under Christian instruction, did he receive a visit from a man-of-war ship.

He was driven from his mission station, and had to live in a native hut, under the protection of a heathen tribe; but there was neither inquiry by, nor support from, representatives of great military powers. It mattered not.\* His confidence was expressed in the words, "The Lord is our refuge and strength: therefore will we not fear!"

The exception referred to is hardly worth naming; for it was a French vessel that called—not to ask what it could do for the missionary, but to inquire what the missionary could do in the way of giving information about a boat, with crew belonging to a French vessel, that had gone to sea, and been heard of no more.

During the first year of the work, when his life was in danger, and help from man could not be expected, and, therefore, was not sought, a chief came on his own initiative, and walked about the house night after night, carrying a loaded gun, and every now and then blowing his pans-pipe, to break the monotony of the still hours. That same man proved, at a later period, his personal opposition to the Gospel by threatening to shoot the missionary! † His act of rendering protection to Mr. Michelsen was in obedience to an impulse which no one could account for, except by concluding that, for the moment, he was doing God service without knowing it.

---

\* Specially gratifying were the visits, in 1890 and 1891, of H.M.S. *Dart*, with Captain Frederick and his noble officers. Whilst cruising about in the Group, to render any necessary assistance if called upon, the object of the visits to Tongoa was of the most pacific character—namely, adjusting the charts. Captain Frederick is no less a faithful servant of the Lord Jesus, than of her Imperial Majesty; and it was to him a profoundly greater joy to witness God's victory over sin and ungodliness, than it would have been to see the Queen's cause triumph over enemies vanquished in martial conflict. The Christian conduct of the Captain and his officers did more to impress the natives with an idea of the greatness of the British Empire, than could have been effected by the thundering of cannon or any other warlike demonstration. † See p. 87.

The natives are not such artless children as some would imagine. A story will show them to be by no means wanting in cunning when they can exercise it to personal advantage. In 1886, during the Tarawera eruption in New Zealand, there was a heavy fall of volcanic dust on Tongoa.

It fell on the mission house at Selembanga during the night with the gentleness of snow, and covered the ground like a thick black carpet. As much as a hundredweight was swept from the iron roof of the mission house. The fact that the dust closely resembled gunpowder suggested a wicked trick to the minds of some of the non-Christian natives.

Some time previously the supply of firearms and ammunition had been stopped at Queensland. Many heathen, having gone to the colony in the hope of laying in a stock of these, returned to their islands much disappointed. Why not pass off upon them as gunpowder some of the volcanic dust? The thought developed into a settled design. Old flasks were filled, and the occasion awaited. By-and-by a ship anchored at Tongoa, having on board some heathen natives of the Solomon Islands and other groups to the north. Tongoans boarded her, and offered the dust for sale as gunpowder.

The "returns"—men who had served in connection with the labour traffic—were ready to pay any price for that which would give stilts to their pride on rejoining their people. They gave axes, knives, calicoes, tobacco, pipes, and anything else the Tongoans asked for; and for a time were satisfied with their bargains. If in the end there was dissatisfaction, there is the consolation that the "ammunition" did nothing worse than proclaim the folly of those who bought it, and the knavery of those who sold it.

Kanaka "returns" have not always been well paid. The temptation has been to load the men with trinkets instead of giving them substantial recompense. A native of Tongoa, on one of the Fiji islands, received with much gratification a roll of bright-coloured wall-paper, which he thought was "calico." Going to a great feast, he cut off a piece and "clothed" himself—according as the fashion is for such to attire themselves. When the time to dance arrived, and the festive round caused profuse perspiration, the man's finery ill became his noble figure. First it hung to him; and at length it left him.

It need hardly be said that the man's want of shrewdness afforded the best part of the evening's entertainment, and taught all the lesson of not depending too implicitly on European honesty. Indeed, the natives have to-day a not very complimentary term in their vocabulary; "white heathen" with them designates all Europeans who are not "missionaries," *i.e.*, God-fearing persons. Yes; such is the truth. God-fearing visitors to Tongoa, whether traders or naval officers, are by the people called "missionaries."

Before leaving the island on furlough in 1891, Mr. Michelsen intimated his willingness to baptize a few believing natives. Among the candidates were two old men who answered to the description of the two who, in the parable, went up into the temple to pray—"the one a pharisee, and the other a publican."

One of the two, of quiet demeanour, said he desired baptism. He was asked: "What about your sins?" "Oh," he replied, "I have no sins."

"But," inquired the missionary, "how was it with you before I came?" The benighted man said: "I have always been as I am now—just as you see me."

"But have you not sinned?"

"No."

"Well then, I am sorry to say that Christ is not for you: Christ only came to save sinners."

All that Mr. Michelsen could say failed to convince this man that he was a sinner. He endeavoured, however, to make it plain to him that baptism was only for such as had gone to Jesus for salvation from their sins.

The other candidate had been a "sacred man," whose former life was well-known to the missionary, and had been anything but sinless.

"What about you?"

"Ah! I have killed men; I have eaten men; I have stolen; I have been guilty of witchcraft; and, indeed, I do not know what wicked thing I have not done." After a brief pause, the penitent continued: "My son is a Christian, and so is my daughter. I am an old man, and perhaps may not live until you come back again. My heart cleaves to the Lord; and I want to confess Him as my only Saviour."

This man had not attended the course of regular instruction required of candidates; but the missionary had no doubt as to his duty to baptize one who could make such a confession. "This man went down to his house justified rather than the other." He belonged to Panita, the first station of the mission. He long did business as a "sacred man" throughout the island. The people soon learned, however, that the missionary could deal more effectually with their sicknesses. Losing his trade, the man went to a neighbouring island to "practise." When Christianity was introduced there, he returned to Tongoa. His business having entirely gone, he realized his need of Divine consolation, and threw in his lot with the Christians. His son, a very fine young fellow, is one of the worthiest believers on the island.

That young man, Taviroto, spent some time in Queensland; and, amongst other occupations, he served a milk-dealer. On returning to the island, he stayed at the Mission House. On one occasion he saw Mrs. Michelsen setting the milk-dishes. He wanted to know why she had not put the water in! In the simplicity of his heart he thought the milk-dealer's practice in Queensland was the correct thing, rather than an expedient to increase his profits.

There has been considerable discussion among Christian workers in the South Seas regarding the way in which believers should "show the Lord's death till He come." With the natives wine is a drink passing under the general name of "grog," against which the missionaries utter loud and constant warnings. What wine was in the East, the milk of the cocoanut is in the South Seas.

The question has, therefore, been asked, May not the cup of remembrance be filled with the grateful drink for which the Christians cannot but be thankful to God, in preference to the beverage which, as imported from abroad, is a noxious mixture of chemicals, coloured and strengthened to suit an acquired taste? The "cup of blessing" may, in the opinion of some workers in the islands, very appropriately contain that drink which is practically the native substitute for "the fruit of the vine." The Communion rite would, it is maintained, lose nothing of its significance by the oriental wine being replaced by its New Hebrides counterpart—the milk of the young cocoanut.

The question remains an open one. Mr. Michelsen tells of a native boy who, relating to some acquaintances what he knew of Christianity said, "They have a 'holy eating,' at which they eat bread and drink grog." The heathen thought this a grand feast; and it must be capital to be a Christian, so as to have the special privilege of drinking the grog against which the missionaries warn them. Rev. Dr. Inglis held that cocoanut-milk is the wine of the islands, and should have the preference.

There are three distinct languages spoken in Mr. Michelsen's district—the Tongoan, which is the same as that spoken on Nguna; the Makura, which is not so widely used; and the Tasiko, which is one of a family of languages, and is spoken on Epi, Malekula, and Ambrim. All have been reduced to writing with the Roman character.

In the Nguna-Tongoa tongue nearly the entire New Testament has been translated. In this Rev. Peter Milne has been a devoted and laborious worker. Two small books have been written by Mr. Michelsen in the Makura language, also some hymns. Since then, he has decided to encourage the use of Tongoan among the Makura-speaking people. In Tasiko the Gospel according to Matthew, as translated by Mr. Michelsen, has been published by the British and Foreign Bible Society.

When the Otago Synod granted the missionary leave to visit Europe, in 1891, the Mission Committee was authorized to collect money to facilitate the journey. The mission funds were, however, already so strained, that nothing could be advanced. Except for money from some other quarter, the workers could not have left their sphere. The natives, out of love to Mr. Michelsen and his wife, speedily solved the difficulty by making arrowroot of the value of £100 to pay the passage. This is no isolated act of generosity on the part of the Christianized natives of Tongoa.

Asked with what interest, or otherwise, the Tongoans have listened to the Gospel message regarding the return of the Lord Jesus, Mr. Michelsen said : " To the natives the prospect of Christ's coming again, and the hope of the Resurrection life, is most charming. When they report the death of believers, it is in the words that he or she has 'fallen asleep.' Everything is very material with them—very real ; and they expect the higher existence to be substantial, because they cannot so well realize any other. They hope for the life of the world to come; and look forward to Christ's coming as 'the blessed hope.'"

It is cheering to witness the tenacity with which some of the native converts "hold on to their Book"—that is, stand by the Word of God and pursue the Christian life. There are many stories of native steadfastness, even on the part of such as have, for a time, left the Islands. Moreover, worldly sailors, who have ridiculed and jeered at the natives while on the voyage to Queensland, have afterwards confessed to the failure of all endeavours to put some of them to shame. It is the joy, if not the boast, of such converts to say, "I am not ashamed of the Gospel of Christ."

The young man Timataso, who at one time called himself "Missis," and ultimately became the leading chief on Tongoa, should have a place among converts who have regarded themselves as "saved to save." As a youth of sixteen, he went to Queensland, about the year 1884; that is, before "recruiting" from Tongoa had been prohibited. The missionary was then residing at Selembanga, and was not so well informed as he could have wished to be of how the young man was faring among his heathen friends at Lumbukuti. As a fact, the teaching he had received in the early days of the work at Panita, had taken a deep and ineradicable hold of his soul. In Queensland he fell in with some natives of the bush village of Pélé, which was at that time at war with Lumbukuti. Not affected by this, Timataso availed himself of the opportunities that were afforded him of preaching the Gospel to these heathen from his own island. At least, in one instance, the blessing of God attended his efforts. A Pélé young man returned from Queensland a decided Christian; and when, in course of time, a teacher was settled in the village, he proved a great help in the work.

After some years, this young man disappointed the missionary by accompanying a number of his people to Port Mackay in Queensland. The reason of their action was afterwards made clear—they were dissatisfied with the conduct of the young chief of Pélé, who did not give to Christianity the support which he had promised his people to do. The missionary was, however, agreeably surprised to receive, some months later, a letter from a young man, a European, engaged as a clerk in a sugar plantation office at Port Mackay. After referring to the Godlessness of the white men by whom he was surrounded, he mentioned that on a recent Sunday he noticed a number of Kanakas loitering about a large shed on the plantation; some were playing jews' harps, others concertinas, and for the most part all were amusing themselves in various ways. He observed, however, that there was a steady current flowing into the shed, and so he went to see what the attraction was. He there found a company of newly-arrived Tongoans, and a number of other islanders, listening to the preaching of a young Pélé man, who proved to be none other than Timataso's convert. The people were listening eagerly to the message of salvation. Comparing the conduct of these "savages" with that of the Godless Europeans around him, the correspondent was deeply impressed by the scene.

There is neither brook nor water-shed on Tongoa, and the rain is quickly absorbed by its pumice-stone subsoil. As a rule, the water required for domestic purposes is obtained from a few insignificant springs, which, however, are not to be depended on in dry weather. At times want of water has been a serious trouble. Mr. Michelsen saw the need of sinking a well, and advised the natives to undertake the work. As a beginning, to make sure of finding water, they set to digging near the sea-shore. They soon got what they need not have dug for—salt water. It required some encouragement to induce them to work further inland. They were at length induced, and their enterprise was richly rewarded. To their great joy and astonishment they came upon beautiful water.

"That's what 'the Light' does for us!" was the spontaneous remark of several. "Only think," they went on, "that we have more than once so suffered from want of water, that we have nearly died; and yet here it was all the while, a short distance under foot!" The Tongoans praised God—accepting the well as a gift of his loving Providence. Mr. Michelsen was careful to explain that the water was the free gift of God; and now the people of Tongoa needed to "thirst" no more, for though other springs should fail, here all might drink of the life-sustaining supplies.

Not only does "the Light"—the Gospel of Christ—give to the Tongoans a well of water like unto Jacob's, of which they may drink, to thirst again; but it is destined to give to the dwellers on continents, as well as islands, access to "the well of water which springeth up into everlasting life."

# APPENDIX.

## The New Hebrides Mission.

READERS of these pages will be interested by some general account of mission work in the New Hebrides. For many of the facts I am indebted to Dr. Steel's work, "The New Hebrides and Christian Missions."*

Pedro Fernandez de Quiros, a Portuguese navigator, was the first European to discover one of the New Hebrides Islands. On April 10th, 1606, he sighted the north end of a land which he supposed to be Australia, and called it Tierra Australis del Espiritu Santo. He sailed into the large bay. The port was called Vera Cruz; the river flowing into the bay he called the Jordan, on the banks of which he *commenced* to build the "New Jerusalem."

Captain Cook, however, was the real discoverer of the Group. His surveys were so near the truth that a good deal of the present chart of the Group is constructed on his drafts. It was in 1774 that this great English navigator sailed twice through the Group and discovered and named them all.

Many accounts have already been given of Christian Missions in our Group; and yet with regard to the deeds of cruelty, stories of danger and sorrow, as well as the power of Jesus to save, even among these cannibal savages, it may well be said, "the half has never been told." We propose to give a brief description of the Mission from island to island.

* Nisbet & Co., 1880.

## Appendix.

ANEITYUM is the most southerly island in the Group. In 1845 Samoan teachers were settled there. Rev. John Geddie and his wife went in 1848. It is not easy to express opinions of the qualifications of a man whom one has not seen at work; but my impression is, that a greater pioneer missionary never settled in the New Hebrides. In 1852 he was joined by the scholarly Dr. Inglis. Whilst we would by no means forget much valuable work of translation done by Dr. Geddie, and also by Mrs. Geddie and Mr. Copeland, Dr. Inglis, after twenty-five years' careful toil, was able to present to the people of Aneityum the complete Bible. When Dr. Inglis arrived, the natives, then some 3000, were open to receive teachers in every district of the island. After many a hard battle with heathenism in the early days, the question had now changed from "who will have" to "who can give the Word of God to the people?"

Dr. Geddie died in 1872, esteemed and loved by his fellow-missionaries, and lamented by the natives. Rev. J. D. Murray, also a Canadian, became his successor. He was compelled, though with much reluctance, to retire in 1876, owing to his wife's ill-health. Rev. Joseph Annand, M.A., was appointed to the station in 1877; Mr. and Mrs. Annand had previously laboured some four years among the heathen on Efate. On leaving the mission field in 1877, Dr. Inglis was succeeded by Rev. J. W. Lawrie. The worthy doctor was afterwards kept busy for a considerable time with the printing of the Aneityumese Bible, and died in 1891. After a period of labour on Aneityum, Mr. Annand took up a new station on Santo, and the entire charge of Aneityum was left to Mr. Lawrie.

FUTUNA. — Whilst Aneityum presents high hills and deep valleys, and is, generally speaking, clad with the richest growth of trees and plants, Futuna seems to be one square coral rock, lifted some 2000 feet up out of the sea. The natives are a race very different from the Aneityumese, and probably came to their island from the east, centuries after Aneityum was peopled. Rev. John Williams, the martyr of Erromanga, visited the island in 1839. In 1841 Rev. A. W. Murray settled the first Christian teachers. In 1843 one of these with his wife joined the army of martyrs, being slain and feasted on; and the others were cast over the rocks into the sea. In 1853 teachers were sent from Aneityum; and, thirteen years later, Rev. Joseph Copeland, with his wife, arrived on the island. In 1876 Mrs. Copeland died, and Mr. Copeland's health failed. He has not since been able to take up regular work on Futuna. After many trials, sorrows, and much patient toil, he could not say that the people had renounced heathenism; yet they seemed "not far from the Kingdom."

The island remained without a European missionary until 1883, when Dr. William Gunn and Mrs. Gunn were settled there. Although teachers had been at work since Mr. Copeland left, the mission evidently declined during the interval; so that Dr. Gunn found the situation almost as difficult as if the people had been altogether heathen. Faithful labours are now beginning to bear fruit. A church has been formed, and it seems as if the worst of the battle with heathenism is past.

TANNA.—A magnificent island, fertile and beautiful. A volcano of exceptional activity makes it peculiarly interesting to the traveller. It is peopled by some 8000, the sturdiest natives in the New Hebrides. It is difficult to say why, but it is a fact that Tanna has cost more mission work, probably, than any other island in the Group, with the least apparent results. The first native teachers were placed on Tanna by John Williams on November 18th, 1839. One of these died, and the other two were removed to Samoa.

Messrs. Turner and Nisbet were the first missionaries, but had to escape for their lives in 1843. From then till 1858 no European missionary was located on the island. In 1853 small-pox was introduced from California, and did fearful work both among the Tannese and native teachers. In 1858, Revs. J. G. Paton and J. Copeland (afterwards on Futuna as already stated), also Revs. J. W. Matheson and S. F. Johnston, were settled on the island. In 1859 Mr. Copeland left to take charge of Dr. Inglis' station, on Aneityum, during his absence. In three years, Messrs. Johnston and Matheson, Mrs. Paton and child, and Mrs. Matheson and child, were dead. It has been said, however, that both Mr. Johnston and Mr. Matheson were in ill-health before they went to the island. Mr. Paton also had a good deal of fever; and the scenes of death and sorrow around him, besides considerable difficulty with the natives, made up a very sad chapter in his life. At length he considered it necessary to flee. Mr. Johnston died suddenly in 1861. Seven years later, Rev. Thomas Neilson, an able and prudent man, settled at Port Resolution, near Dr. Paton's old station, but in a much healthier locality. He held the fort there under many difficulties ; but his cool courage fitted him peculiarly for dealing with the bouncing Tannese. He laboured on till 1882, when he retired ; and has since been labouring in Victoria. He suffered much from asthma, on account of the damp climate ; and it is also probable that the sulphur fumes from the volcano had to do with his illness.

In 1869 Rev. William Watt took up a station near the place where Mr. Matheson had lived. Mr. and Mrs. Watt do not rejoice in the same amount of success as some of the other missionaries in the Group ; though, of late, their endeavours have been attended with considerable encouragement. But they have done what no one else has done in the New Hebrides ; and, perhaps, a similar case is hard to find anywhere else in the world. They have held out against the heathenism of Tanna, and their lives have frequently been in danger now nearly a quarter of a century ! Mr. Neilson's former station is now worked as an out-station under Mr. Watt. On the north-east of Tanna, north of the volcano, is the station occupied by Rev. William Gray. He commenced work in 1882, and has been making slow, but sure, progress from the beginning. In 1891 he reports an attendance at school of 80. The missionaries who occupy Tanna do not despair of success. Let us pray for them, and with them, that they may soon rejoice in a great harvest ; that we may see fair Tanna, with the proud Tannese, at the feet of Jesus.

ANIWA is a low coral island which can only be seen a few miles away. It is not more than some twelve or fourteen miles from Port Resolution, on Tanna, Dr. J. G. Paton's first station. The population is now not above 160 souls. Rev. T. Heath, of Samoa, settled teachers there in 1840. They were afterwards re-inforced by teachers from Ancityum. One of these was killed. In 1866 Dr. Paton settled on the island. The work went forward steadily from that time ; and in two years nearly the whole population was nominally Christian. It was not long ere the island was placed beside Ancityum as a Christian island.

As Dr. Paton's fame as a mission lecturer has gone long before these pages, and will go where this short account will never reach, it is needless for me to add that it was judged that his time would be better spent moving about interesting the Churches in the New Hebrides Mission than to remain on Aniwa among a small and decreasing population. Since 1881 he has been labouring with indefatigable zeal, advocating the Mission cause. The Mission is indebted to his efforts for very large sums of money collected for Mission ships. Aniwa has since been taken care of by Mr. Watt.

ERROMANGA.—After all, there is, perhaps, no island in the New Hebrides so interesting to the Christian Church as this. We shall pass over Captain Cook's difficulty with the natives, and the dread chapter of the sandal-wood traders, which preceded, and was probably connected with the martyrdom of Williams and Harris. Erromanga is one of the larger islands, though by no means the most fertile in the group. Its bare table-lands give it a beauty of its own; and, indeed, it is quite a relief after visiting the other islands, so luxuriantly clad with tropical vegetation, to see the large expanse of open grass-covered land, with here and there a solitary tree. One almost feels impelled to ask: Where are the cattle and the farmhouses?

The scene on page 32 shows the sand-bank on the other side of what is now called the Williams River. It was there that John Williams and Harris went ashore; and, not very much further up, that they were slain. They were carried up a short distance, to nearly opposite the tall cocoanut palm; there their bodies were divided between the various parties who had shared in the deed of blood and ignorant revenge. This would lead some to second the statement of Dr. Steel, that "the natives are the lowest of the tribes inhabiting the New Hebrides." But I certainly differ here. Erromanga has produced some noble men, and almost every missionary north of Erromanga has to acknowledge that the best servants he had were Erromangans. Doubtless, they take more polishing than any of the natives of our Group who were before them brought under the influence of Christianity and civilization.

In May, 1840, Rev. T. Heath, of Samoa, settled teachers on the island; but, after much suffering and danger, they had to be removed the following year. Some years afterwards several young men were got away to Samoa, and placed under Christian instruction. They were sent back to their island, but the success of the experiment is very doubtful. Native teachers must have the support of a European missionary, if they are to succeed among the heathen. Rev. G. N. and Mrs. Gordon (of Prince Edward Island) took up residence on Erromanga in 1857. Four years later they were murdered. Their graves are found on the other side of the river. It is worthy of note that the first man to step forward to take the fallen soldier's place was his own brother.

Rev. J. D. Gordon reached Erromanga in 1864. He found some who had not forgotten the instruction of his brother. But, on the whole, the island was still heathen. Rev. James M'Nair, from Scotland, joined him three years subsequently. Though spiritually and mentally well equipped for the work, he evidently was not physically fitted for life in malarial regions. In July, 1870, he slept in Jesus. His dust rests beside that of Mr. and Mrs. Gordon. Plots were laid against him, and in all probability he would have been killed. But he did not live long enough to be registered on earth among the martyrs of Jesus Christ. Rev. J. D. Gordon, burning with love for the perishing, opened a station also on Espiritu Santo, where his prospects of success were very good; also on Erromanga the Word made a decided impression among some of the people. Mr. Gordon was even aspiring to leaving his bones on New Guinea. This, however, was not granted him; for in March, 1872, he was also called upon to join the great company of martyrs, being tomahawked. Having just finished revising the 7th chapter of Acts, in like manner as did Stephen he "fell asleep."

The same year, Rev. H. A. Robertson and Mrs. Robertson (also from Canada) arrived. They expressed a wish to be settled on Erromanga. The story of a missionary with his young wife volunteering to set up their home as witnesses for Jesus on the isle where lay the bones of their six predecessors, is too pathetic for me to attempt to dwell upon it. Their lives have often been in the greatest danger. The Lord has rewarded their courage and faith; and nearly the whole population, some 2000, are professedly Christian.

EFATE is a large, beautiful, and in most parts fertile, island in the middle of the Group. The first news of a Saviour was taken to Efate by some Christian natives from Samoa, who had lost their bearings in their canoes on the ocean. They first landed on Tongoa,

### Efate and Nguna. 179

where several of them were slain; others escaped, and settled on Efate, where they began to tell the story as best they could. In 1845 the first teachers were sent to the island, by the London Missionary Society's agents, from Samoa. They passed through dangers and difficulties; but, more or less regularly, the work was kept up, and considerable progress was made. Rev. D. Morrison, a Canadian, was settled at Erakor, on Efate, in 1864. Two years afterwards, Rev. James Cosh, M.A. (now Dr. Cosh, Balmain, Sydney), arrived at Epango. He had to retire, after a comparatively short period of work, on account of his wife's health; but he is still affectionately remembered by the natives. Dr. Steel informs us that both these cases of illness were due to residing in a close grass house. I quite believe it, and sincerely trust the day is not far distant when grass roofs in tropical countries with a moist heat will cease to be used as residences for missionaries. The natives use these roofs; but as *they* often have fires in their houses, it is by no means so unhealthy in their case.

In 1872 Rev. J. W. Mackenzie, Nova Scotia, a pattern missionary, whom no one can know without loving, settled at Erakor. With zeal, love, and wisdom, he and his energetic wife have continued the work with great success up to the present. Mr Mackenzie's health has not always been what he might desire, and therefore his work has been more difficult than otherwise. It is a wholesome thing for any missionary to pay a visit to this station. In 1872 Rev. D. Macdonald, from Victoria, took up work at Havannah Harbour. He found his field utterly heathen. After some years of patient effort, however, an impression was made, and now there are very few heathen in the district. Mr. Macdonald, who is still in the field, is an untiring student of New Hebrides languages, and has published several books about them.

NGUNA.—The story of the mission on this island, if well told, would be second only in our Group to that of Erromanga. The opposition of the heathen, the raging of the enemy, deeds of cruelty and murder, personal danger to the missionary and his wife, make up a chapter of almost unparalleled missionary experience. Indeed, if Rev. Peter Milne had had his own way, he would have been settled on Erromanga; and it is very likely that his name would have been added to the long list of the martyrs of Erromanga.

# Appendix.

He arrived in the islands in 1869, and remained on Erromanga with Mr. M'Nair until the next year, when he was settled on Nguna among some of the most determined cannibals in the New Hebrides. Mr. Milne seems to have a love for adventure, but does not see much in it after it is over. In his open boat he visited islands far and near; Pélé, Kakula, Emau, Mataso, Makura, Emae, were all visited by him. Indeed, all the islands north of Nguna, including also those now in my district, where the

MISSION CHURCH AT NGUNA.

same or a similar dialect to the Ngunese is spoken, were considered as his district *pro tem*. He therefore paid a visit in his boat to Tongoa and other islands—a distance of upwards of thirty miles. With all his nautical enterprise and hard work—for a greater worker never joined our Mission—Mr. Milne was plodding for many years without seeing much fruit in the way of heathen turning to Christ. Translating was done, and thus a great work of preparation got through, which inevitably would bear fruit in its season.

At last the ice broke, and after the first hundred souls were gathered in, the work went forward steadily and surely. He has now seven islands in his district, with nearly 2000 Christian natives and very few heathen. He has probably more nominal Christians and more baptized natives than there are on the four southern islands put together. One of the most magnificent sights I ever enjoyed was to see the Nguna church packed with worshippers as close as they possibly could be ; even then many had to sit outside. Mr. Milne is now about 58 years of age ; but I do not think he has more thought of retiring from his post than has the most youthful member of the Mission.

Of course, we pass over the story of the TONGOAN Mission, which has already been told at some length.

EPI is the next island in the order we follow. The southern part was in some measure influenced from Tongoa from the very commencement of my work there. The first attempt at regular effort on this island was made by Mr. Holt and his wife, who were settled at Mburumba, on the west side of the island in 1880. He was a man bent on winning souls, and the mission was in a most promising state even after a few months' work. At the end of the year his house was burned down, and resort was had to an open reed structure, which brought on fever. That, along with other circumstances, led to Mr. Holt retiring in 1881. The next year Rev. R. M. Fraser took up the work near Mr. Holt's station, though in a less healthy locality. He has since been labouring with great success.

On the north side of the island Rev. T. Smaill, B.A., was settled in 1890. There never was a mission station that gave better promise of success in so short a time. There is reason to expect that very soon the whole population on Epi will be Christian. Humanly speaking, there seems to be nothing wanting to hasten that happy day, beyond a good staff of teachers sent out over the whole island.

AMBRIM is to the north of Epi. We can only hope that the bright chapter of this mission is to come. In 1883 Rev. W. B. Murray, B.A., was stationed there under the falling dust of an active volcano. The people were friendly ; the missionary and his wife were possessed of such qualities and attainments, mentally and spiritually, as would lead one to anticipate a certain success among a people apparently open for mission work. But our hopes, and theirs, were sadly disappointed. On his way to the island, Mr. Murray took a cold which settled upon his lungs. At the end of the next year he was compelled to retire. He died the year after in New South Wales, and his widow returned to Scotland with double sorrow. She had to leave behind not only the husband to whom she had bound her life, but also the work she loved so well.

In 1885 Rev. Charles Murray, M.A., went out with his young wife to take his brother's place. They also entered on their work most cheerfully and hopefully. The next year Mrs. Murray died at Futuna (Dr. Gunn's station). Mr. Murray returned to his station and remained there a year; but he suffered so severely with fever that a removal to a cooler climate was deemed absolutely necessary. On both occasions I led in prayer at the service of settlement, and I still believe that a great blessing is in store for Ambrim. A teacher has been in charge ever since; but very little progress has been made. In 1892 Rev. Robert Lamb, M.A., B.D., M.B., C.M., was settled on the island. We know not if he is to be privileged to be the reaper. Let us unite in praying that the thousands of heathen on Ambrim may soon be guided into the safe harbour. There are rocks ahead. At least one Roman Catholic teacher has found his way to the island, and French traders are also there.

MALEKULA is to the west. I wish I had a more cheerful account to give of this mission. Revs. A. Morton and T. W. Leggatt arrived in the Group in 1886, with their young wives, and were settled at their respective stations the next year. The work of house-building, translation, and itinerancy has been carried on by these zealous and able missionaries; but the reaping is only being done to a very limited extent. Death, sickness, and plots, are sad chapters from the short history of the mission on Malekula. Mr. Leggatt is now labouring there a lonely widower, and it is a matter about which there are divided opinions if Mr. Morton is right in remaining on the island with his wife's health seriously injured by the many exciting scenes they passed through in their dealings with the heathen.

Rev. John Gillan was also settled on a small island off the coast of Malekula in 1889. He is not without some encouragement; but it is not easy to say, after so short a time, what his present efforts may lead up to. Natives often lead a missionary to the brightest expectation; but when he gets so near to them that it becomes clear that they cannot have both sin and Christ, the difficulty arises.

MALO.—Rev. J. D. and Mrs. Landels, who arrived in the Group in 1886, were settled on this island of about 3000 inhabitants in 1887. The Word is evidently taking root, and everything looks hopeful. Some have already been baptized, and a considerable number are attending school and Gospel services.

SANTO.—In 1887, Rev. J. Annand, M.A., and Mrs. Annand settled on the small islet of Tangoa, on the south side of Santo. This is the third time they have begun mission work in the New Hebrides. They are Canadians, and are worthy companions of their countrymen who have distinguished themselves so much in the New Hebrides Mission.

Mr. Annand's reports are always on the safe side; but even he says (*The Christian*, November 24th, 1892), "To all our visitors our success here seems real. Certainly to outward appearance our natives are doing fairly well. On Sabbath no persons visit their places of labour. Neither fishing nor hunting is now thought of, but the house of God is frequented. A very fair percentage of the people attend the services." Rev. A. H. and Mrs. Macdonald began work at a station a considerable distance up the west coast of Santo, in 1890. The people seem hearty, and his report in 1891 was most encouraging. But what are two missionaries among probably 30,000 cannibals?

The missionaries engaged in work in these Islands meet once a year in Synod, to deliberate upon the internal working of the Mission. This is by virtue of powers vested in them by the churches represented in the Mission. These are: the Presbyterian Church of Canada; the Free Church of Scotland; and the Presbyterian Churches of Victoria, New South Wales, New Zealand (North), Otago (N.Z. South), South Australia, and Tasmania.

## The Islands and the People.

Rev. Dr. Lamb, who has undertaken work on the island of Ambrim, has lately made two tours of the Group, making the acquaintance of nearly every white person, settlers and missionaries. In a descriptive letter from Nikaura, Epi,* dated July 26th, 1892, he says :—

"Our first impressions were not wholly favourable. A warm welcome met us at every door of house or hut; but most of the white faces that first greeted us seemed those of men and women who had just returned from the grave, so white and emaciated were they. It was the end of the hot season—an unusually hot one—and *La Grippe*, along with fever (malarial), had been prevalent. Still, there were a few who were looking well, and some who, as yet, have not known what fever means. These were the exception. The universal experience, so far, has been that the roses of health, which bloom in other lands, are doomed to wither in these islands. The deep black soil, with rank vegetation, is for us a steaming hot-bed of fever and ague. But the fever is mild, seldom causing more than weakness and emaciation, from which, with the proper remedies, recovery is rapid. Settlement and cultivation, letting in the air and sunshine, may ultimately dispel the miasma; but much muscle must waste, and many lives be expended before that condition will be achieved.

"The islands are truly beautiful; but their beauty has been just sufficiently overpraised to deprive one of the delight of surprises. There is variety and contrast; beaches, black and white, flat islets and lofty mountains, still lagoons and foaming reefs, reeking swamps, and glowing, rumbling craters. Nor is the vegetation everywhere quite alike. Ambrim and Aoba are vast gardens of cocoanut palm. Tongoa and Epi are specially the home of wild creepers, which overtop the tallest trees, and bury all, except the towering palm, beneath one green mantle. All the northern islands are covered by dense tropical forest, in which the banyan is king; while the shade is beautified by a luxuriance of ferns and many-hued crotons. The Group, as a whole, is volcanic; the soil in the south is somewhat barren, and the land more open. Towards the north Nature is more bountiful, and there is abundance of deep black mould. Already a trade has sprung up in coffee of the finest quality, in copra, and maize. Cotton, tobacco, and

* Extracted from *The New Zealand Presbyterian*, Dunedin, Oct. 1, 1892.

sugar-cane grow admirably. Bananas—some thirty species—arrowroot, pineapples, oranges, lemons, chilies, the custard apple, peanuts, and ginger, grow without cultivation. Yams, taro, sweet potatoes, and the bread-fruit, are among the staple products of the native gardens. Some of our common vegetables and grasses, when introduced, flourish well. Cattle, goats, pigs, and possibly sheep, thrive, as do all our domestic pets. Some kinds of *bêche de mer* abound, and there are plenty of fish, though the natives are but poor fishermen. Kauri, a hard wood like teak, and a light durable wood that seems to resist the white ant, are among the timbers. These islands are of great value, destined to be a garden of tropical fruits and spices. . . .

"To judge from the action of the Queensland Legislature, which has staked its reputation on the advantages to be reaped from the labour traffic, one would suppose that the natives too were a valuable race. It is the very poverty and abjectness of the Kanakas that make them such valuable slaves to the sugar-planter. Once removed from their own island, nay, their own particular district, few of them, in their present condition, are capable of exhibiting either stamina or independence. Of twelve lads removed by a labour-ship from Erromanga last year, ten are already reported dead.

"The New Hebrides and sister Groups form a strange chapter in the study of human history. Here life is at its lowest ebb, and the people as the washed-up foam and *débris* at the margin of sand and wave. The jet-black and the much-coveted nut-brown complexion are found members of the same small village. A single islet is the home of Malay and Papuan. In the New Hebrides alone there are some thirty different dialects, needing almost as many versions of Scripture. The Aobans are fair-skinned and clean; their neighbours, the Ambrimese, are black and filthy. Here on Epi there are three main dialects, and those who speak one are foreigners to the rest. Every village, though comprising only five or six huts, is an independent unit; and, according to its size, is strong or weak, the friend or foe of its neighbours, fearing and being feared. There is no such thing as a natural death; if a man die, it must be due to *kimi*\* (a kind of witchcraft), and the suspect is shot; war and devastation follow. True, there are many specimens of the noble savage; but the people as a whole are of a low type, and are falling a prey

---

\* The *Kaimasi* of Tongoa. See page 119.

to the violence of their own superstitions, and to disease, constitutional and parasitic. Besides the contagious and epidemic diseases introduced by whites, or brought back from the colonies—viz., 'specifictinea,' scabies, whooping-cough, measles—there are native elephantiasis, consumption, bronchitis, and a form of struma almost universal, manifesting its nature in offensive abscesses, glandular swellings, and ulcers of skin and bone. Great is the multitude of Lazaruses, with no pitying dog to lick their sores. The people need to be better housed, clothed, and fed. Despite the loss of the picturesque in native dress, which follows the introduction of European clothing, and which ethnologists deplore, the people absolutely need some simple garments to enable them to withstand the effect of the rapid changes of their own climate. Let some lover of the picturesque devise a garment that will combine simplicity and taste.

"Here we have had a capital rest while planning and preparing for another step in advance. The mission station is built on a spur, which, beyond the reed enclosure and a cluster of cocoanut palms, drops down 250 feet into the sea. The scenery is equal to any in the Pacific. Right at our feet is an immense fringing reef, on which the billows unceasingly break in milk-white floods with deafening roar; which, re-echoed from the mountain slopes, and blending with the rustle of the palms, suggest on a pitchy night the presence of Alpine heights and rushing torrents. To the right and left are wooded bays and headlands, also fringed with reefs; and right in front stands Lopevi, an almost perfect cone, 5000 feet high, down whose slope the black lava pours sheer into the ocean. From the centre of the crater a thin column of smoke or steam curls upward, warning the few inhabitants of a slumber that may any day give place to activity, as happened ten years ago, when the refugees on this very shore were clubbed and eaten by their professed friends. To the right of Lopevi is the open sea, and to its left is Paama, with Ambrim in the background. The face of Nature changes with every passing hour. The colours of the sea, the gorgeous cloud scenery at sunrise and sunset, the weird effect of black shadow and silver glow chasing each other on the surface of the deep on a cloudy moonlight night—all are ours just now. We are dwelling amid scenes that dwarf the works of the greatest masters, surpassing them in extent and magnificence as Nature can surpass Art.

"Last Saturday, a small party, we went down to the shore to

picnic and to see the coral reef. The tide was low, and we could go a long way out. With old shoes to protect the feet, and armed with a hammer and cold chisel, we waded about peeping into the pools and knocking off choice lumps of coral. The fish in the pools are small but exquisitely beautiful—green and gold, peacock-blue, pink and white, silver and black, red and green—all colours in almost endless diversity. As for the coral, it is a very different thing from what you see under glass cases. Our attention was first caught by what looked like a rhododendron blossoming in a shallow pool—it was a lovely growth of coral, a pale pink or purple. And then we began to find almost as many colours of coral as of fish—cream-white, emerald, lilac or lavender, dark browns and purples, pale yellows and sky-blues. Within a small area we collected some eighteen different varieties, classifying them according to form. After gathering till we were about tired, we had a delightful time on the beach.

"It has taken me a day and a half, while waiting for the steamer, to boil and cleanse the coral, tubful after tubful being put on the fire. The colours fade rapidly once the polyps are out of the water, and the smell as they die is repulsive. So, to whiten our specimens, we boil them for a few hours in a solution of washing soda, then pour clean water on them from a height, and lastly expose them to the sun and rain.

"On Sunday, the day after the picnic, we had a service in the native-built school-house about 10 a.m. There was a fairly large audience, over eighty in all. It is not easy to speak to natives. You have to do it in concrete terms and very figuratively, or you will not be understood. There is scarcely an abstract term in their languages; they have little or no idea of what is meant by a 'city,' and none perhaps had ever seen a 'lamb,' both of these words being in the text. In the afternoon I accompanied the missionary to a village at some distance along the shore, in the opposite direction to that we had gone on Saturday. We held service on a slope in one of the irregular circles, in the centre of which stood the wooden drums and symbols of idolatry. There were about fifty present. The old chief sat at the feet of the missionary; and his son, a handsome, strapping, intelligent young fellow, recently returned from Queensland, sat on the rock beside me and looked on my book. The Gospel has had a powerful influence on the people, who are now beginning to understand the missionary and look up to him as their friend. Peace is established, and there is comparative safety in travelling. The natives come to barter and to buy medicine and books from villages at considerable distances. Several of these are asking for teachers, and alas! there are none to send. Although there are already 180 such teachers in the field, the one great need of the New Hebrides is more native teachers. Hence the demand for an Institute in which to develop and strengthen for this service the physical, mental, and moral fibre, of the most promising of the native young men and women.

"On our return, we stepped aside to visit a few huts and see some of the sick. At the entrance of three of these kennel-like abodes we stopped and called to the inmates; when, in each case, forth there crawled an old man black with dust and soot, shrivelled, nude, and ashamed of his sores. The oldest case was perhaps the most pitiable. Pardon the description, but the truth must be told. From head to foot he was suffering from a loathsome, contagious skin disease, while from every toe pus was oozing. This hardly seemed the worst feature. He lived within a stone's throw of the sea and was yet so foul that the grey hair seemed rooted in earth rather than in a human scalp. Some one has coarsely remarked that medical and surgical work amongst these people is several degrees below that of a veterinary surgeon; but these savages are, after all, members of the human family—though its waifs—and have the same hope. Capital cases these for the medical missionary to score by!—that is, to exemplify to the native mind in the most telling way, the real nature of the Gospel of Christ. Let no one infer that nothing has yet been done for them. The Presbyterian Church throughout the world has sent into this field men and women who for half a century have sorrowed and wept with the heathen in their degradation, seeking to raise them to better things, not without much success. Perhaps the most striking though silent witness to this is the fact that nearly every mission station has its own little graveyard. There are churches and congregations here that put to shame many a colonial settlement. Still, much remains to be done. Every missionary is doing more or less medical work; but as Christianity has founded its free hospitals in every civilized community, so the necessary complement of the teaching here given is a similar institution."

## Works Published by Morgan & Scott.

**THE EVANGELIZATION OF THE WORLD.**
A MISSIONARY BAND. A RECORD OF CONSECRATION, AND AN APPEAL.
By B. BROOMHALL,
*Secretary of the China Inland Mission.*
Contains Three Maps and numerous Illustrations and Portraits.
Cloth Bds., 2s. 6d.; Bev. Bds., Gilt Edges, 3s. 6d.
"This is a most remarkable book. . . . It is one of the most powerful appeals for Foreign Missions issued in our time, and altogether perhaps the best handbook that exists for preachers and speakers in their behalf."
*The Church Missionary Intelligencer.*

**DAYS OF BLESSING IN INLAND CHINA.**
AN ACCOUNT OF MEETINGS HELD IN THE PROVINCE OF SHAN-SI.
Compiled by MONTAGUE BEAUCHAMP, B.A.
*With an Introduction by*
J. HUDSON TAYLOR, M.R.C.S., F.R.G.S.
With Illustrations and Maps. Cloth Boards, 1s. 6d.

VOLUME I. NOW READY.

**THE STORY OF THE CHINA INLAND MISSION.**
By GERALDINE GUINNESS,
*Author of "In the Far East."*
With Introduction by
J. HUDSON TAYLOR, M.R.C.S., F.R.G.S.
In Two Volumes. Cloth Boards, 3s. 6d. each.
Illustrated with Coloured Maps, Portraits, and Pictures.

**PUNROOTY:**
OR, THE GOSPEL WINNING ITS WAY AMONG THE WOMEN OF INDIA.
By CLARA M. S. LOWE.
Cloth Boards, 2s. 6d.
"We have been charmed by this book. We could not lay it aside till we had read it through. Exciting as a novel, it stimulates a reader's faith, prayer, consecration, and love of souls."—*Star in the East.*

**CHINA'S SPIRITUAL NEEDS AND CLAIMS.**
By J. HUDSON TAYLOR, M.R.C.S., F.R.G.S.
With numerous Illustrations and Diagrams;
Conspectus of Protestant Missions in China, &c.
Paper Covers, 1s.; Cloth Bds., Gilt Edges, 2s. 6d.
"The story of faith and work told in it should be read by every earnest Christian. It is a mine of wealth for the missionary speaker and deserves a prominent place in missionary literature."
*Wesleyan-Methodist Magazine.*

**WORKING AND WAITING FOR TIBET.**
A SKETCH OF THE MORAVIAN MISSION TO THE WESTERN HIMALAYAS.
From the German of H. G. SCHNEIDER.
Translated and Revised by ARTHUR WARD.
With Illustrations.
Paper Covers, 1s.; Cloth Limp, 1s. 6d.

**IN THE FAR EAST.**
LETTERS FROM GERALDINE GUINNESS.
Edited by her Sister.
New and Enlarged Edition—Profusely Illustrated.
Bound in Ornamental Paper Boards, 3s.;
Cloth Boards, 4s.
*With Introduction by*
J. HUDSON TAYLOR, M.R.C.S., F.R.G.S.

**THE WORK OF AN EVANGELIST.**
A REVIEW OF FIFTY YEARS LABOUR.
By Rev. A. B. EARLE.
Tinted Covers, 6d.; Cloth Boards, 1s.
"A very interesting little work, by the author of 'Bringing in Sheaves.' . . . We have here much in little. The views of this aged worker are worthy of serious consideration."—*King's Highway.*

**BRINGING IN SHEAVES.** A RECORD OF EVANGELISTIC LABOURS.
By Rev. A. B. EARLE.
*With Biographical Sketch of the Author.* Tinted Covers, 1s.; Cloth Boards, 1s. 6d.
"There is much in this volume that could not fail to stimulate and encourage. It is prefaced by a singularly interesting sketch of the author, who appears to be a man of remarkable devotedness, combined with great earnestness."—*Preacher's Lantern.*
"Local preachers will find this book just the thing to help them in their work, and to all such we earnestly recommend it."—*Primitive Methodist.*

★★★★★★★★★★★★

London: MORGAN AND SCOTT, 12, Paternoster Buildings, E.C.
*And may be Ordered of any Bookseller.*

# PUBLISHED BY MORGAN AND SCOTT.

## Biographical Works.

**FIDELIA FISKE:**
THE STORY OF A CONSECRATED LIFE.
By REV. W. GUEST.
Tinted Covers, 1s.; Cloth Boards, 1s. 6d.;
Cloth Elegant, Gilt Edges, 3s. 6d.
"Here is truth stranger and more thrilling than fiction, the incidents of a missionary career which are to the glory of God and of His truth."
*The Sword and Trowel.*

**MARY LYON:**
RECOLLECTIONS OF A NOBLE WOMAN.
By FIDELIA FISKE.
Tinted Covers, 1s.; Cloth Boards, 1s. 6d.
"Among American educators Mary Lyon occupies a first place. The book is a study for teachers; and still more for all who wish to exercise spiritual influence over others, consecrating their work as teachers to the noblest ends."—*The Freeman.*

**DUNCAN MATHESON:**
THE SCOTTISH EVANGELIST.
HIS LIFE AND LABOURS.
With Life-like Portrait.
Tinted Covers, 1s. 6d.; Cloth Bds., 2s. 6d.
"The life of a real man, consecrated in life and full of zeal for the Lord. This biography will not only interest, but benefit a wide circle of readers." ... We are right glad to see so worthy a memorial of so worthy a man."—*Sword and Trowel.*

**THE CHRISTIAN HERO:**
MEMOIRS of ROBERT ANNAN of DUNDEE.
With Two Illustrations.
Tinted Covers, 1s.; Cloth Neat, 1s. 6d. CHEAP
EDITIONS; Tinted Covers, 6d.; Cloth Boards, 1s.
SPECIAL CHEAP EDITION for Gratuitous Distribution, 4to size: Tinted Covers, 1d.; 7s. per 100.
"From first to last this volume is full of interest, and valuable lessons are deduced from the life of this humble but honoured servant of Christ."
*Word and Work.*

**JOHN WESLEY:**
HIS LIFE AND TIMES.
With Portrait. By J. W. KIRTON, LL.D.,
Author of "Buy your own Cherries."
Tinted Covers, 6d.; Cloth Limp, 1s.;
Cloth Boards, 1s. 6d.
"In some nineteen chapters Dr. Kirton tells in a popular and fascinating style the Life of the great founder of Methodism. It is emphatically the biography of Wesley for the people."
*Primitive Methodist.*

**GEORGE WHITEFIELD:**
A LIGHT RISING IN OBSCURITY.
With Portrait. By J. R. ANDREWS,
Barrister-at-Law.
Tinted Covers, 6d.; Cloth Limp, 1s.; Cloth
Boards, 1s. 6d. PRESENTATION EDITION: Cloth Boards, Gilt Edges, 5s.
"The popular and powerful preacher, whose efforts synchronised with those of the Wesleys, is here set before us in a striking piece of portraiture; and the extracts from his diaries give many life-like touches to the sketch."—*Publishers' Circular.*

## WORKS by D. L. MOODY.

The late Rev. C. H. SPURGEON said:—
"There can be no need for us to commend the living, blazing speech of our brother Moody. Who can equal him in natural simplicity, all aglow with holy passion!"

**POWER FROM ON HIGH.**
OR, THE SECRET OF SUCCESS IN
CHRISTIAN LIFE AND CHRISTIAN SERVICE.
Tinted Covers, 1s.; Limp Cloth, 1s. 6d.;
Cloth Boards, 2s. 6d.

**TO THE WORK! TO THE WORK!**
A SERIES OF TRUMPET CALLS
TO CHRISTIAN SERVICE.
Tinted Covers, 1s.; Limp Cloth, 1s. 6d.;
Cloth Boards, 2s. 6d.

**FULL ASSURANCE OF FAITH.**
SOME THOUGHTS ON
CHRISTIAN CONFIDENCE.
Limp Cloth, 6d.; CHEAP EDITION, 2s. per doz.

**PREVAILING PRAYER.**
A SERIES OF ADDRESSES ON PRAYER.
Tinted Covers, 1s.; Limp Cloth, 1s. 6d.;
Cloth Boards, 2s. 6d.

*A Complete Price List of all Mr. Moody's Works may be had post free on application to the Publishers.*

LONDON: MORGAN AND SCOTT, 12, PATERNOSTER BUILDINGS, E.C.
*And may be Ordered of any Bookseller.*

# PUBLISHED BY MORGAN AND SCOTT.

## Works for Bible Students.

### THE BIBLE REMEMBRANCER.
#### A Handbook to the Old and New Testaments.

*With Steel Frontispiece and 12 Maps.* Containing a large amount of valuable Biblical information.

Tinted Covers, 1s.; Cloth, 1s. 6d.; Cloth Boards, 2s.

"We do not know a more useful Handbook for Bible readers and Bible students. It seems to embody nearly everything necessary in such a book."—*Christian Commonwealth.*

### THE TABERNACLE, THE PRIESTHOOD, AND THE OFFERINGS.
#### By HENRY W. SOLTAU.

*With Four Beautiful Coloured Illustrations, and numerous smaller Engravings.*

Cloth, 5s.; Cloth, Bevelled Boards, Gilt Edges, 6s.

"The work is full of teaching, spiritual, and far reaching; and we have much enjoyed reading it."
*The Sword and Trowel.*

### SEARCHING THE SCRIPTURES.
#### In Order to Abiding Communion with God.

Also Suggestions for Bible Readings and Study; and a Plan of Consecutive Daily Reading.

By Dr. J. ANDERSON, M.R.C.S.

Tinted Covers, 1s. 6d.; Cloth Boards, 2s. 6d.; Cloth, Bevelled Boards, Gilt Edges, 3s. 6d.

"Preachers and teachers will find it a treasury of thought, beautiful expositions, and fruitful suggestions. The volume is nicely got up, and is suitable for a prize or a present."—*Oldham Chronicle.*

### "THE CHRISTIAN" BIBLE READINGS.
#### Notes and Readings on the Five Books of Moses.

GENESIS. EXODUS. LEVITICUS.
NUMBERS. DEUTERONOMY.

Tinted Covers, 1s.; Cloth Limp, 1s. 6d.; Cloth Bds., 2s.; Cloth, Bev. Bds., Gilt Edges, 2s. 6d.

"A series of useful notes to accompany the reading of the Pentateuch. If any of our Bible-class friends should be thinking of studying this part of God's Word, they cannot do better than accept the guidance proffered them in this volume."
*The Quiver.*

### CHRIST AND THE SCRIPTURES.
#### The Living Word and the Written Word.

By Rev. ADOLPH SAPHIR, D.D.

Tinted Covers, 1s.; Cloth, 1s. 6d.; Cloth Bds., 3s.; Cloth, Bev. Bds., Gilt Edges, 3s. 6d.

"The book is full of thought, and palpitates with life. It is admirably adapted for the mature and thoughtful; but it is peculiarly fitted to give a right direction to the thoughts and lives of young, earnest, and inquiring persons."
*Newcastle Daily Chronicle.*

### NOTES ON BIBLE READINGS.
#### A Collection of over Six Hundred Subjects.

By S. R. BRIGGS and JOHN H. ELLIOTT.

Tinted Covers, 2s. 6d.; Cloth, Bevelled Boards, Gilt Edges, 3s. 6d.

"A book which every Bible student should possess ... And those who conduct Bible Readings will find it most suggestive."—*Christian Progress.*

### IN THE VOLUME OF THE BOOK.
#### Or, The Pleasure and Profit of Bible Study.

Being an Introduction to the Study of the Holy Scriptures.

By Rev. G. F. PENTECOST, D.D.

Tinted Covers, 1s. 6d.; Cloth Limp, 2s.; Cloth Boards, 2s. 6d.

"No one can read this almost unique volume without being stimulated to a more diligent study of THE BOOK."—*Night and Day.*

### MANY INFALLIBLE PROOFS.
#### The Evidences of Christianity; Or, The Written and the Living Word of God.

By Rev. A. T. PIERSON, D.D.

Tinted Covers, 2s.; Cloth Boards, 2s. 6d.; Cloth, Bevelled Boards, Gilt Edges, 3s. 6d.

"For half-a-crown any one may obtain here all that is best in the way of fact and argument on prophecy and miracles; on the scientific accuracy and the ethical beauty and sublimity of the Bible; and on the Person and teaching of Christ."
*Methodist Recorder.*

---

LONDON: MORGAN AND SCOTT, 12, PATERNOSTER BUILDINGS, E.C.
*And may be Ordered of any Bookseller.*

EVERY THURSDAY.          PRICE ONE PENNY.

# The Christian.

### A WEEKLY NEWSPAPER

Containing Accounts of Christian Work and Missionary Enterprise in all Parts of the World.

**ORIGINAL ARTICLES, NARRATIVES,**
    **POETRY, NOTES ON PASSING EVENTS,**
        **And GENERAL EVANGELISTIC INTELLIGENCE.**

With Portraits and Biographical Sketches of Eminent Christian Men and Women.

*Extract from a Letter from a Missionary in China:—*

"For some time past I have regularly received from an unknown friend a copy of 'The Christian.' I should like the kind sender to know how welcome the gift comes to one living in the interior of this land, far from European society and Christian intercourse."

*Extract from a Letter from a Missionary in India:—*

"Your most interesting and valuable paper is really very edifying and strengthening to believers of all standards, to the weak and strong alike."

> On receipt of Postal Order for 1s. 8d., The Christian will be forwarded to any Address in Great Britain, direct from the Publishers, post free, for 13 weeks.

EIGHT PAGES MONTHLY.      PRICE ONE HALFPENNY.

# The Herald of Mercy.

### AN ILLUSTRATED MESSENGER FOR HUMBLE HOMES.

*Each Number consists of Eight Quarto Pages, with Full-page Illustration and several Smaller Engravings.*

Containing
**STIRRING APPEALS, NARRATIVES,**
        **PAGES FOR THE YOUNG,**
                **CHOICE EXTRACTS, &c., &c.**

"Full of short, telling anecdotes; rich in encouragement, comfort, and solemn warning. They point to Christ and His unsearchable riches. The Illustrations are good and suggestive."—*The Friend.*

> Eight copies of "The Herald of Mercy" will be sent post free to any Address direct from the Publishers for 12 months on receipt of P.O. for 4s.

LONDON: MORGAN AND SCOTT, 12, PATERNOSTER BUILDINGS, E.C.
*And may be Ordered of any Bookseller or Newsagent.*

www.ingramcontent.com/pod-product-compliance
Lightning Source LLC
Chambersburg PA
CBHW030820190426
43197CB00036B/709